Did you know that many older women prefer dating men younger than themselves? If you're a younger man who wants to get started dating older women, this book shows you how to get a handle on the crucial differences between older and younger women. Learn how to approach, and get involved with, older women, find out how to push back against the public disapproval that older woman-younger man relationships attract, and discover the real reasons why many older women prefer younger men. Based on the author's dating experiences with older women.

HOW TO DATE OLDER WOMEN

Andrew Dolan

HOW TO DATE OLDER WOMEN

ISBN 978-1-4357-2073-2

Lulu Press
860 Aviation Parkway
Morrisville, North Carolina 27560
U.S.A.
www.Lulu.com

TABLE OF CONTENTS

CHAPTER ONE
Getting Involved
With Older Women

What Do You Know About Older Women?

Maybe you've heard rumors about what older women are supposed to be like. Older women are supposed to be sophisticated. Older women are supposed to be sexually experienced and open to sharing the fruits of their experiences with the right kinds of younger guys. Older women are supposed to be wise in the ways of the world and men. Older women are supposed to know how to make a relationship work out just right for everybody involved. Older women are supposed to know how to really take care of a man. Older women are supposed to be able cook just like mom, possibly because many of them are moms. These sorts of things that you've heard are parts of the mystique about older women, and this mystique is a mosaic, meaning a composite impression of different bits of information you've picked up here and there over the years. Older women are

1

generally supposed to be a lot of things, but some of those things might or might not be true for a particular older woman. Some older women might be right for you, others might be right for some other guy and some might not be right for anybody you know. Everybody's different.

If you're not looking to have children of your own, older women are definitely merit your consideration as romantic possibilities, depending on just what the age of the particular older woman you have in mind might be. Most women who are ready, able and willing to have children have done so by the age of thirty-five or so. After age forty, women are rarely able to have children, even when they use fertility drugs. By the time most women reach their mid-forties, their children are starting to move out, go to college, get jobs and get married themselves, leaving mommy presiding over a nest that is getting emptier by the day. Over half of all married women eventually get divorced, making some of those nests even emptier.

Something about getting divorced makes older women who choose to remarry following a divorce get remarried to men younger than themselves at a rate seven times greater than the rate at which women marrying for the first time tie the knot with younger men. Marriage is preceded by dating, and sometimes dating necessarily involves women dating several different men of different ages until they find someone with whom they click. Some women, especially those who have had particularly nasty divorces, would not even consider getting married again, but they do want to date again, because they are looking for sexual companionship with a hedonistically hormonal dimension. Either way, whether they want to get remarried or not, many divorced older women will often turn out to be receptive to certain types of younger men. (Shehan)

How Many Older Woman-Younger Man Couples Are There?

Dating and marriage statistics back up the idea that older woman/younger man couples are part of a growing trend. Over half of all marriages end in divorce, often by age forty. One study showed that in the United States, 34% of women age forty to sixty-nine surveyed turned out to be dating men younger than themselves, and 7% of them were dating men ten or more years younger than themselves. (Mahoney)

Marriage statistics for the United States show that 7.2% of marriages involve couples where the wives are four or more years older than their husbands, a total of 4,307,000 men. In addition, 4.1% of marriages involve couples where the wives are six or more years older than their husbands, a total of 2,451,000 men. (Census Bureau)

Among unmarried couples living together in the United States, 14.6% are cohabiting couples where the women are four or more years older than the men, a total of 738,000 men. In addition, 9.1% of cohabiting couples involve women who are six or more years older than the men, a total of 450,000 men. (Census Bureau)

183,000 men in the United States are married to women twenty or more years older than themselves, and another 19,000 men are living with women twenty or more years older than themselves. (Census Bureau)

In summary, a total of over five million men in the United States are either married to, or living with, women four or more years older than themselves, and a total of almost three million men are either married to, or living with, women six or more years older than themselves.

In Canada, four percent of married couples involve wives four to six years older than their husbands. One percent of married couples involve wives seven to nine years older than their husbands, and another one percent of marriages involved wives ten or more years older than their husbands. (Boyd and Li)

Older Women May Be Good For Your Health

One study showed that younger men who married older women actually lived longer than men who married women within a few years of their own age. There are several possible reason for this. One reason might be that the older women sampled chose to marry younger men who were generally healthier than average. Not very surprisingly, men who start out healthier usually live longer because they were predisposed to live long and healthy lives in the first place, regardless of whether or not they happened to get married to older women. Of course, being married to an older woman might offer additional health benefits, such as improving heart-lung action through years of nightly sexual marathons, an enjoyably hedonistic method of longevity improvement. Maybe home cooking had something to do with their longevity as well. (Kemkes-Grottenthaler)

Exactly What Age Makes
A Woman "Older?"

"Older" is a comparative adjective, and one part of the comparison involves the man in a relationship. The younger a man is, the greater the degree to which an age difference of only one or two years can make a woman appear subjectively "older." A college freshman might be inclined to see a college junior two years older than himself as "a lot older." By contrast, a forty year old man might be inclined to see a woman two years older than himself as "not really older." Beauty and comparative "olderness" thus exist primarily in the minds of the beholders.

Marriage statistics typically classify marriages between people who were born within three years of each other as being age-homogamous, which means that people born within three years of each other are statistically close enough in age to be categorized, both by each other, and by the rest of the world, as being about the same age. The same principle applies to dating.

A woman who is one to three years older than the man she is dating is not generally considered "older," in part because she does not look older than the man does, and might even appear a bit younger if she is in somewhat better overall health than the man with whom she is involved. Couples embodying age differences of three or fewer years do not usually attract any attention at all when they go outside and walk down the street, though a few particularly nosy people who spend all of their spare time trying to keep tabs on what everybody in the neighborhood is doing might be able to spot minor differences in age at a glance and chatter about it all day long.

Sociologists, psychologists, marriage statisticians and the general public agree that a woman is "older" than a man, in the sense that their age-heterogamous relationship is outwardly discernible and considered noteworthy (at least in the minds of some people), where an age difference of about five, or more, years is present. The more years a woman has on a man, the more people are likely to be able to immediately spot their age difference and thereby take notice of that relationship. The reason that people usually start taking notice of age-discrepant relationships where the woman is five or more years older than the man in the relationship is because she often appears to be visibly older. The rule of thumb is that an age difference of five to ten years will get a woman colloquially categorized as looking "like his older sister." A woman who appears to be something like ten, fifteen, or more, years older than her boyfriend (or husband) will start getting colloquially categorized by the general public as looking "almost old enough to be his mother." There is an unacknowledged psychological reason that the general public will often unconsciously choose to use the terms "sister" and "mother" to characterize age-discrepant relationships where the woman is visibly older than the man.

Adults do not need permission from other people, or the general public, to enter into a relationship with an older (or younger) adult individual. Consenting adults can do what they feel to be right for themselves with other consenting adults without regard for what other people, meaning the general public, think. The consent of the general public is neither needed by age-discrepant couples nor should it become an issue for members of such couples at any point in time.

A private relationship between two adult individuals necessarily excludes a need for public opinion polls, in the sense of asking casual strangers on the street for "approval" to get on with an age-discrepant relationship. Feeling the need to do so is characteristic of a non-adult mentality.

There is no such thing as an adult woman being "too old" for a younger adult man, because there is no universal or objective rule that applies to adults as regards age-discrepant relationships. It always comes down to somebody or other's subjective opinion. Adults can make up their own minds about what is right or wrong for themselves. While it is true that some people might say that a particular woman is "too old" for a particular man, this is simply their subjective opinion about what they would be likely to do in that person's place, and the opinions of those with whom you both disagree with and do not care to interact with are inherently meaningless because they do not reflect your opinions. If you feel good about being involved a particular woman, your opinion and her opinions are the only opinions that count. Other peoples' opinions are no reason to do or not do anything, because they are nothing more than throwaway opinions. If you feel good about being involved with her, get on with it, even if other people don't like the fact that you like being involved with a woman who is visibly older than yourself. You'll never feel good about yourself if you do what other say you should do with your life. They don't have to notice what you are doing, and you don't have to notice them or their opinions. He

9

who pays the piper should call the tune. You are the one paying the bills for your relationships, so call any tune you want you feel like hearing, and dismiss those playing tunes you have chosen not to pay to hear.

Why Get Involved With Older Women?

Each man has his own private set of extremely personal, and usually undisclosed, reasons why he likes whatever sort of women he happens to like, and why he does not care for other types of women. The key is compatibility, that simple word that covers a universe of subjective psychological ground. One man's definition of compatibility will often turn out to be another man's definition of incompatibility. The elements of compatibility include sexual, emotional, physical, social and intellectual components, and different men are looking for completely different customized mixes of those elements.

Men who have dated and married older women often mention that certain things about older women operate to attract them and maintain their interest. The first factor is that older women, especially divorced women, don't make a habit of playing the sort of mind games that younger women play all too often. Older women are more likely to say what they really think and are less likely to care about what other people – meaning their parents, neighbors and girlfriends – think about their relationships. When an older woman likes someone, she will just try to get on with a relationship and not waste her time with adolescent games or ask other people what they think of a particular man.

A lot of younger women try to keep younger men guessing about what they are really thinking, and many men, younger and older, find such behavior to be a definite turn-off. It is also worth noting that some older men who have dated younger women have been known to say that they will never make that mistake again, because differences in psychological maturity levels can make it hard for them to maintain such relationships on anything beyond the superficial level. It takes two to make an adult couple.

Younger men who have been involved with older women often mention that sex is "better" with older women, "better" meaning more enjoyable for them, than sex with younger women. Women who have been married, or have been in several long-term relationships, have a lot of sexual experience under their belts, have put the fumbling stage of sex behind them, are more confident about making their sexual preferences and interests known to their male companions and use their past experiences to guide how they screen in the sorts of men they might have reason to believe are sexually compatible while screening out the sorts of men they have reason to believe are not sexually compatible.

Finally, some older women see being in a relationship with a younger man as a chance to take up residence in a sexual candy store and gorge themselves on sexual sweets every night. If an older woman knows how to take care of a man, there are younger men out there who will respond positively to what those older women have to offer.

Younger men who have dated and married older women often mention that older women are nicer than younger women. Older women often have a lot of experience in relationships and know more about how to make them work than do younger women with limited dating experiences, and no marital experiences, to their names.

It is the equivalent of the difference between a rookie baseball player and a well-seasoned pro. Their batting averages differ because they have been playing the game for different lengths of time. The more you play a game, the better you get at playing that game.

Why Older Women Seek Out Younger Men

Older women are often heard to say words to the effect that they like being involved with younger men because those younger men make them feel "young" or "younger." These are shorthand terms that some women use to characterize their emotional and sexual response to being involved with younger men. Being with younger men might take such women back, psychologically speaking, to the way they felt when they were younger. Being with younger men might also bring back memories of their experiences with men back when both parties were overflowing with the raging hormones of youth. Whatever the details of their characterizations of how being with younger men makes them feel, at the bottom of their mental water well is a psychological repository of enjoyable emotional and sexual memories and fantasies.

Some older women enjoy being with younger men because women who have been married for extended periods of time understand immediately how men are likely to behave at a certain age, and may prefer men who exhibit age-specific behavior with which they already have experience. For example, a forty-five year old, recently divorced woman has good memories of what her husband was like at different points in time during the course of their twenty-five year marriage. When she meets a younger man who is twenty-five years old, she will remember what she and her husband did right (and wrong) during their relationship at that age, and she has a pretty good idea of what another younger man in that age range is like, how he is likely to treat her and how she should treat him.

Getting involved with a younger man who is ten, twenty, or even more, years younger is thus more than trip down memory lane for an older woman. It is also a sort of a second chance to get it right, in the sense that she knows what to do right, and what to avoid doing wrong, when she gets involved with a younger man of a particular age. Women who want to make relationships work will try to do so based on their memories of personal experiences when they were certain ages, and, to a lesser extent, based on what they have heard from other women about what made the relationships of those other women work back when they were of a certain age.

Younger men are generally physically healthier and more energetic than men old enough to be their fathers, though older men who work at staying fit and healthy are quite easy to find. The key difference is that younger men take good health for granted, while older men who are healthy and energetic are likely to be in good physical condition because they have consciously worked at keeping themselves fit and healthy. Some do, some don't.

Younger men have generally had fewer negative life experiences that have older men, and may bring a fresher, less jaundiced outlook on life to relationships with older women. Older women have had plenty of troubles of their own, and do not need extra servings of somebody else's problems added to their plates.

A sense of humor on the part of younger men will almost always be welcomed by older women. Older women like men of any age who do not take themselves too seriously, and are capable of seeing daily life from a humorous perspective.

Women of all ages prefer men who know what they want and what they do not want, and won't be changing their minds every fifteen minutes about major issues. If you know what kind of person you are, you will communicate what you are more effectively than will someone with no sense of self-definition. The more assets you bring to a relationship, the better off both of you will be.

Is Dating Older Women A Fetish?

Critics who do not share the sexual interests that some men have for women in certain age ranges are prone to designate those men whose interests they do not share as being "fetishistic," or having a "fetish," while at the same time designating their own idiosyncratic interests with a label other than that of fetish. Anything that is even slightly out of the ordinary can easily wind up being labeled as a "fetish" by critics, except when those critics indulge in such things themselves. Critics consider everybody else to be a bit odd to the degree to which they are unlike the critics. Therefore, almost anything can be designated as a fetish by a critic as long as the critic doing the designating does not share that fetish, at least at that very moment. When those critics take on that interest themselves, they give a label other that that of fetish.

When large numbers of people do something or agree on something, it becomes mainstream, normal and okay for almost everybody. Different types of men seek out different types of women for relationships, and they do so without regard for public opinion polls. If a man prefers blondes, redheads, green-eyed women or some other physical type, that is his business. If a man prefers women ten or twenty years older than himself for a mixture of reasons that include the sexual, his preferences are a good thing for him, even if a public opinion poll were to show that most other people disagree with his choices.

In the final analysis, the only people that a man really needs to poll about the propriety of entering an age-discrepant relationship is himself and his female companion. Public opinion polls concern only public people and public issues. Private opinion polls are for private people who poll only themselves about their opinions, and their polls are reserved for internal, private consumption only, meaning the consumption of the two people in the relationship. If other people don't like the fact that two adults involved in a one-on-one relationship are not inviting third parties to join in their private opinion poll, and couldn't care less about what those other people think, those other people don't have to notice, they just need to move on and let the two people involved in an age-discrepant relationship get on with enjoying themselves. If it makes you feel good, do it, even if other people say that it should not feel good because they are of the personal opinion that it is not right for you.

Incidentally, normal people who lead normal lives don't like being called ambulatory fetishes because they happen to be blondes, redheads, have green eyes or are older than the men that they are involved with. People, and groups of people with common characteristics, are not fetishes. For that matter, one man's supposed fetish is another man's girlfriend or wife.

The Right Sort Of Older Woman For You

Everybody has their own extremely idiosyncratic definition of who is "right" for them. Individual preferences lead to individualistic choices that make no "sense" to any one else because individual preferences are designed exclusively for individual consumption, and not for public consumption. Your private opinion regarding what you prefer in a woman is not intended for public consumption or public approval. This means that the extent to which you alter or water down your individual preferences to suit anybody other than yourself, the lesser the degree to which your choices will meet your individual inner needs and satisfy you. Your life thus should not be set up to make sense to other people, but rather to make sense to you and only to you.

Your inner needs do not change because other people hold the opinion that you should to change them to suit their opinions. Your inner needs result from your lifetime-to-date choices about what you like and don't like to see in other people, and these choices are presumably tempered by experience. Socialize with new and different types of older women, see what you like, and stick with it until your new experiences accumulate to the point of showing you that you should stay involved with those new types of women.

There is a simple way to test whether a particular older woman is right for you, or simply a passing fancy or infatuation. When you are involved with an older woman who meets your sexual, intellectual, social, emotional and other needs, the greater the degree to which she meets your needs, the greater the degree to which you will find yourself not noticing, and not thinking about, other women. If your needs are already being met with a particular older woman, you won't feel a need to notice other women.

Obviously, different women offer different mixes of attributes and characteristics. One woman might attract you in a primarily sexual way. A second woman might attract you in a primarily intellectual way. A third woman might attract you in a primarily social way. Each particular woman exerts a different sort of attraction over you. Another man who has different preferences might see those three women completely differently with respect to his own set of idiosyncratic preferences. This is an oversimplified example, of course. Every woman is multidimensional and exhibits a mix of sexual, intellectual, social and other characteristics, and is not just an all-or-nothing monodimensional stick figure.

The important thing for you to do is to thus to keep an eye on how you react to a particular woman. If you find yourself constantly comparing a given woman along one or more dimensions or characteristics in an unfavorable way to one or more other women, she is probably not a suitable long-term match for you, and may not even be a suitable short-term match for you.

If you do not find a woman physically attractive enough to excite you, you and she are unlikely to have any sort of future together, regardless of how wonderful her social skills or intellectual prowess might turn out to be. A woman who fails along any primary dimension will not be able to keep your interest for long, so take note of any sort of mounting subconscious discontent with her along any major dimension. Almost anything goes if you are excited by someone, and nothing goes if you are not excited by someone .

No woman that ever lived is perfect for you. Men and women have to adjust to each other when they get into long-term relationships, because matches are never perfect. Sometimes, however, the two of you will mentally gloss over each other's imperfections when your hormones fan the flames of mutual passion.

If there is a particular thing that you constantly fantasize about finding in an older woman, be it a particular type of figure, a quirk of personality or educational attainments, make a point of seeking out women with the trait, or traits, that you fantasize about. Make yourself known to older women who embody those traits. Some of them may be looking for a younger man just like you.

The only way to find out whether or not dating an older woman is right, nor not for you, is to do it. It might turn out to become a natural part of your life, or it might turn out to be an idea that was right for some guy but not for you. Either way, whichever conclusion you come to should be a conclusion based on real-world experiences, not theorizing, fantasizing or both. At some point you have to either do it or wind up never going it at all. Doing anything now necessarily requires making something of a break with the past. You don't have a lot of guidelines, and have even less experience, at dating older women, so the only thing to do is to go about getting involved and find out first-hand what older women have to offer.

Why Age Differences Attract Certain People

Some people have a well-defined interest in whatever might be new and different for them, though those same things may not be new or different for many other people. Some people, for example, like to visit foreign countries during summer vacations. They visit foreign countries precisely because those countries are foreign to them and differ in a variety of ways from their customary abodes in their home countries. After spending a number of years visiting foreign countries, they slowly develop marked preferences, such as a preference for the cuisine and architecture of certain Mediterranean countries.

What a tourist considers an exotic foreign land is neither exotic nor foreign to those who call that "foreign" country their home, of course. It is only "different" by comparison with what has come before for a given individual, and might not be very "different" at all for somebody else who happens to be a native of that country.

Some people slowly come to realize that a country that was once foreign to them is actually the home that they feel that they "belong" in. Such people might emigrate to another country because they feel that they "belong" there. This feeling is a realization that has usually grown within them, slowly and subconsciously, over the course of time.

Feeling that you "belong" in a country or in a life situation other than the one to which you are accustomed is common enough. This is why people think about seeking out things that are new to them (like older women). What is less common is taking action to emigrate, transplant oneself or otherwise relocate oneself to whatever sort of life situation it is that you feel that you "belong" in.

People who don't take such action to rearrange their lives often wind up going through the rest of their lives feeling like fish out of water. They may be able to keep their lives going on what seems outwardly like an even keel, but inwardly they know that they are simply hollow vessels going in circles without carrying cargo of any importance. They should be doing something different, but are not. If you feel that you belong with a woman in a different age range than yourself, migrate and start making that age range your new home for relationships.

CHAPTER TWO
Things You Should Know About Older Women

Why Older Women Are Attracted To Younger Men

Older women who get involved with younger men are likely to be attracted to younger men for one or more common reasons. In many cases, it's a package deal, in the sense that it is the total package of physical and mental characteristics, instead of any one single thing, that attracts an older woman to a younger man.

First is the physical/sexual dimension. On average, younger men are more likely to be in better health than older men, and their sexual capacity is more likely to not have become impaired. It is quite common for women over forty to describe men in their own age range as sexual "duds," meaning that they consider such men to be wet firecrackers incapable of going off with a bang after women try to light their fuses. Not all older men are like this, of course. As a general rule, however, men who make a habit of not exercising, make a habit of filling up on fatty, greasy and sugary foods, make a habit of smoking and drinking and make a habit of not getting enough sleep, those men are the sort of older men who are most likely to have physical/sexual problems due to poor general health.

A man of any age who is overweight, does not get enough sleep, loads up on fare such as hamburgers and fries on a regular basis, and never gets any exercise worthy of the name is likely to become a sexual dud. When men's hearts, lungs, body muscles and hormones have been in decline for a long time, no other outcome is possible.

The younger a man is, the less likely he is to have gradually accumulated a variety of such health problems. The better his overall health, the better his sexual capacity will be and the more likely it is that women will notice, and react positively to, what a healthy younger man has to offer.

To put it bluntly, some older women are looking for sexual thrills that will make them dizzy with delight, and such older women think younger men are the men most likely to be able to bring sexual thrills their way. This is particularly noticeable in women who are past the age of menopause. After menopause, women no longer need to worry about pregnancy, childbirth and related issues. They can just enjoy the pleasurable aspects of sex without regard for matters such as pregnancy that may have been cause for concern and sexual inhibition when they were younger.

Some older women just prefer the personalities of younger men. While every younger man is different, younger men as a group are more likely to have an enthusiastic outlook on life in general and sex in particular. Their sexual hormones are still raging, and they are also less likely to have excess baggage in the form of cumulative negative experiences that can operate to make them less fun to be with. Older women who have been around the block a couple of times are good at sniffing out men who have developed negative attitudes about life in general and women in particular. The more negative a man's thinking, the less he will have to offer a woman looking for an exciting relationship.

The other side of the coin is that the more positive a man's attitude towards women in general, regardless of whether he is younger or older, the more readily women will sense that he can bring something to a relationship other than unwanted baggage from previous relationships. Attitude counts. While a very small number of women might see a sourpuss as a challenge to win over to their way of thinking, most will see little in such men beyond the prospect of more bad experiences of the sort that they have been trying to put behind them, particularly so among divorced women.

Then there is the very real, but elusive, concept of complementarity. People who do not seem – at least to casual observers – to have much in common, let alone have any prospect of a long-term relationship, have been known to not only get along quite nicely but have even gotten happily married with complete disregard for other people's opinions. The way the two people in a relationship think and talk makes them complementary matches. They have something, or maybe several things, that passes between them and makes mutual attraction and retention their natural state of being.

Intellectual factors can also be important, though this is not necessarily tied to formal education. People who think alike in certain ways will often get along quite nicely. Those with an intellectual outlook on life, in the sense that they are curious about everything going on around them, are likely to have an affinity for others who think in the same vein. By contrast, if one person prefers to play poker every night while another person prefers to visit bookstores, they may be too intellectually dissimilar to have enough in common to keep a relationship going for long.

People Are Psychological Molecules

Older women think about younger men in a different way than they think about men in their own age range, or men older than themselves, and their thoughts guide their interactions with younger men. The other side of the coin is that younger men themselves think about, and interact with, older women in a different manner than is the case with women their own age or younger than themselves.

Differences attract, retain and go on to create something new under the sun. A classic example is the mutual affinity of elemental hydrogen and elemental oxygen for each other. While each element is completely different from the other, the two elements can chemically interact and compound together to form water, something new under the sun that was not strictly predictable if all you knew about the two elements was their separate and distinct chemical natures. When different types of psychological molecules attract each other and create a sphere of mutual affinity and influence, things that were not strictly predictable start to come into existence – like exciting relationships that happen to involve different types of people.

A single musical melody can be enchanting. However, when the interactional musical chemistry between two melodies is just right, playing the two melodies together is a musical form known as counterpoint. When you hear two complementary melodies played together at the same time in counterpoint, they complement each other by creating something new and enchanting under the sun when played together.

Two different types of people bring their own psychological melodies to relationships, and the degree to which they complement each other, in the sense that they mesh together smoothly, is the degree to which their psychological counterpoints mesh together in an effective manner. Age differences yield different melodies that can interact in either an effective or ineffective manner. Different people are looking for different things, and what is a good thing for one man might be much less of a good thing for another man. Human beings are thus human psychological molecules that are best off making contact with a broad array of different types of human psychological molecules so that they can determine by trial and error exactly which types of people offer them the greatest degree of psychological affinity.

Different people have different affinities for different types of people at different ages, in part because they are always changing and learning new things from their experiences. A woman who is age twenty-five might be looking for a man who can fit readily into the role of father of her children, while the very same woman might be looking for a very different sort of male companion when she is age fifty-five, divorced and has children who are no longer a primary concern because they no longer live nearby.

So exactly what are those complementary counterpoints that men and women of different age ranges are looking for in each other?

Sexual interests are at the top, or a millimeter away from the top, on the lists of both men and women. Lots of marriages break up, by the way, because many people, even those who have been married for decades, are simply not sexually complementary, and may never have been so in the first place. Giving birth is rare after age forty, and after divorce, a woman in her forties or fifties would be prone to lose interest in men who embody only such traits as are related to being a good father, especially after the parenthood stage of her life is behind her. Her interests might then shift to men who can satisfy the sexual interests and cravings she may have had to put on hold both during an unsatisfactory marriage to a guy she met when she was nineteen and while she becoming run down while raising a couple of kids.

It is common for women over forty or so to say that men in their own age range are "duds," sexually speaking. While this is, strictly speaking, true for the squeaky wheel who happens to be squeaking away at the moment, is unlikely to be true for the more numerous wheels that are not squeaking away at the moment. Some men over forty are like that, others are not, meaning that you can't generalize about millions of men in an accurate manner, because their sexual performances vary tremendously. The women who chose to get divorced, however, were seriously dissatisfied with their marriages. These are the women you are most likely to meet, and some will tell you at length about the ways in which their husbands turned out to be duds.

Divorced women who remarry get remarried to younger men at a rate seven times greater than women marrying the first time around. Sexual interests are probably a major part of the reason for them remarrying younger men. If a particular woman had an ex-husband who offered her less and less sexual enthusiasm and interest as time went on, she is free to meet her self-determined sexual needs and interests as she wishes when dating, and possibly remarrying, after she gets divorced.

Other factors can also determine complementarity. On a very simplistic level, one person might be a practicing musician and another person might be a practicing music appreciator. One person might like to tell jokes and another person might like to listen to jokes. They might just be two people who like sitting together in front of the fireplace. Whatever the details of their particular mutual form of complementarity, if they feel good about being with each other, they will keep doing it, regardless of whether or not uninformed casual strangers agree that they have the right to be mutually complementary without outside interference. Such couples feel free to feel good about being involved and those who don't agree or understand will simply get left behind in the dust. Those on the inside of the relationship have better things to do with their time.

Older Women Involved With Younger Men Often Have Girlfriends Doing The Same Thing

The loner mentality is more common among men of all ages than among women. Men are more capable of going it alone on different enterprises without feeling any consuming need for social reinforcement approval of their activities from other men (or women). If a man wishes to pursue either a certain career, or a certain type of woman, he often couldn't care less about the nay-sayers.

Women are different than men. A woman who prefers the company of younger men may have to go it alone, but, whenever possible, will seek out the company of other women who also prefer younger male companions. There may be substantial age differences and personality differences between such women, but what brings them together is their mutual agreement on the key point that that younger men are the way to go (for them, at least). They may not see things eye-to-eye on a variety of other issues, but do agree on that one thing, and that decision steers how they craft the other parts of their lives, such as who they can bring their younger male companions to meet without facing a succession of bizarre questions that dance around the issue of age differences without quite hitting the nail on the head.

Women who date younger men do not want to be incessantly barraged by questions about age differences. They instead prefer to get on with enjoying their lives without outsider questioning. They do this by including supportive people, or at least people who are not antagonistic, in their social circles, starting with other women who are also involved with, or looking to get involved with, younger men. They will also attempt to exclude those who are known to be, and those who might become, critical of their relationships with younger men from their social circles, because being forced to listen and respond to critically sneering questions that reek with undertones of jealousy or envy is a waste of time that is better spent on more productive pursuits. No matter how many snappy or critical questions they are forced to waste their time answering, doing so adds nothing worthwhile into their lives.

Most people prefer to keep company with like-minded people, and women who prefer the company of younger men are free to do so as well. Not only are women who date younger men generally supportive of like-minded women, they can also exchange useful tips and bits of information, such as dealing with going out public, the best places to dine, and so on. Younger men who date older women should do the same, meaning that they should seek out like-minded people and exclude critical and hostile people from their social circles. If you're dating an older woman, you don't need to have guys who snicker at you clogging up your life.

Reliable dating statistics can be hard to come by, because nobody goes to the trouble of keeping records about who is dating who, but marriage statistics are collected on a systematic basis. One number does jump out at you from those statistics: divorced women are seven times more likely to marry younger men than are women who are getting married for the first time. Women who marry for the first time most often marry either men close to their own age.

Something about the process of getting a divorce seems to steer older women towards marrying younger men the second time around, assuming that they choose to remarry, and divorce is always preceded by browsing around what the singles market offers by way of dating opportunities. Different types of divorced older women seek out younger men for a variety of individualistic reasons.

Some divorced women had husbands who left them for younger women, or caught their husbands fooling around with younger women, or both. Some women marrying for the first time deliberately marry men older than, or the same age as, themselves, possibly as a result of a parentally-instilled directive to avoid men younger than themselves at an early stage of the game of life. After a divorce, such women see no reason to restrict their field of choices, and some choose to follow the example of their ex-husbands by choosing younger companions. While dating and shopping around after getting divorced, divorced older women may consciously work at avoiding men that remind them in any way of their ex-husbands, and decide to tune into dating younger men exclusively, seeing no reason to take a chance on repeating the same mistake twice.

This can work out in unexpected ways. Some divorced women were previously married to men who were substantially older than themselves, meaning men something like ten or more years older than their wives, and later found that their husbands were having affairs with appreciably older women, meaning women who were often older by a factor ten years or so – appreciably older, in other words. This means that their husbands left them, cheated on them, or both, for women old enough to be the mother of the wives they left behind.

When this sort of thing happens to a woman, it is not hard to see how she could wind up looking down the age ladder for a man at least ten years younger than herself, meaning a man young enough to be her husband's son. Note the prevalence of age gaps in many such broken marriages that seem to cluster the neighborhood of twenty years. Divorces involving husbands who strayed to pursue women with substantial (upward) age differences can often result in the ex-wives of those husbands deciding to try out age-discrepant relationships themselves, since there is no reason for such women to eschew nibbling on what their husbands felt free to sample of freely themselves.

Sometimes you come across older women involved with men substantially younger or older than themselves, and later learn that such women come from family backgrounds where the men, the women, or both, have histories of being in relationships and marriages tilted towards one, or both, ends of the age spectrum, because relationships with people in different age ranges are the norm in such families.

A desire for psychological/social role reversal may partially explain the desire of some divorced women to seek out younger men. After spending years, or even decades, as the chronologically and psychologically junior partner in a marriage that broke up, together with being in a social environment where most women are paired off with men older than themselves, becoming divorced or widowed gives these women a chance to make a clean break with the past.

This includes breaking with the many mistakes that lead to unhappy marriages that culminated in divorce, and allowing themselves to try out something new and different. In some cases, the women may just want to be on top, which they see as a well-deserved change.

Women are subject to a long list of social influences during their formative years that operate to subconsciously tilt them towards doing the socially acceptable "right" thing when dating and marrying. Their parents are often found at the root of the problem. What is considered "right" boils down to what everybody (except the woman herself) thinks is right for her. Their mothers, fathers, other relatives, girlfriends, neighbors and so on tell them to do certain things with respect to men and to avoid certain types of "socially unacceptable" choices that those other people might disdain but which might actually be the right choices for a particular younger woman.

Mother and father don't always know what is best, given that many of them have made messes of their own lives, but feel free to presume to tell their daughters that they should marry a man in given occupation, or some other arbitrary category, ignoring the reality that his personality and outlook on life might be a complete mismatch for their daughter. The parents are always surprised when such marriages end in divorce, but the divorce comes as no surprise to women who have made the mistake of listening to other people when they are the ones who ultimately wound up doing the dirty work of trying to make ill-starred, incompatible marriages work to no avail. There is nothing to be gained from wasting your life trying to make somebody else's unworkable ideas work.

For example, a divorced woman who is age twenty-seven might have been socially conditioned to avoid men younger than herself and to focus only on older men, even if she was actually more physically, meaning sexually, attracted to younger men. If such a woman's marriage to an older man fell apart, such a woman would be more likely to heed only her own desires and opinions the second time around, because having deferred to other people's opinions the first time around completely failed to satisfy her. Those who cannot remember the past are condemned to repeat it, and those who repeat the past will not enjoy repeating the experience the second time around any more than they did the first time around.

As far as younger men are concerned, divorced women as a group offer good prospects to younger men interested in getting involved with older women. Not every divorced woman is open to younger men, but women who have been divorced are more likely than adult women in general to be open to, and to seek out, relationships with younger men.

Older/Younger Cultural Differences

A culture is a widespread way of life shared by millions of people, often within specific geographic boundaries, such as a country where broad segments of the population share substantial similarities. The people within a particular country speak the same language, share many of the same customs, live in a similar manner and generally have many habits and experiences in common. For example, the people of France share a common language, a common culture, a particular outlook on life, similarities of diet, and so on.

Within any large, all-encompassing culture there also exist subcultures that share many of the characteristics of the larger culture while also exhibiting distinctive traits and characteristics peculiar to those particular subcultures that exist within the confines of the larger culture.

A classic example is the difference between residents of cities and farms within a given country. They might speak the same language and live only a few hundred miles apart, but lead completely different ways of life. Subcultures often feature a divergent philosophical outlook on life not found in the larger culture.

To take another example, people who have been in the military have their own modes of dress, slang, way of looking at life, and so on, all of which differ in many particulars from the civilian sector. They have much in common with the civilian sector, but also share a different sort of cultural bond with fellow members of the military. The differences between the military and civilian sectors are so pronounced that there exist military sociologists who spend their entire careers studying the differences between the military and civilians.

People of different age ranges belong to different subcultures because they have had different types of life experiences as a byproduct of growing up, and becoming socialized in, the different social contexts that existed in different eras.

Even members of the same family can be members of different generational subcultures. Brothers and sisters who are as little as ten years apart in age may have gone through very different types of generational life experiences, and their generational life experiences have shaped their personalities, their outlooks on life, how they interact with other people, as well as their attitudes, interests and opinions on a broad range of issues.

We have all been shaped in different ways by the times in which we grew up, and people born before or after us have been shaped in different ways than ourselves. For example, people who personally experienced the economic pinch of the Great Depression are known to have a number of reservations about spending freely that those born just ten years afterwards did not share. Those who grew up during an era of antiwar protests see certain issues differently than those who did not grow up during such an era. People for whom computers have always been around have a different attitude about using computer technology in their everyday lives than those who for whom computers remain newfangled gadgets that they never quite got the hang of using as an everyday appliance, because such devices did not come along until they were well along in years.

The point of this is that, if you are going to date an older woman, meaning someone five, ten, or more, years older than yourself, you need to know a bit about how she grew up in ways that probably differ from the way in which you grew up, depending on how much older than you she is. There may be a lot of things that the two of you do not have in common. She may never have heard of any of the music groups that have "always" been big names to you. Depending on just how much older than you she is, a lot of the music that you think of as oldies were "newies" that she first heard when they were new releases. She may never have heard of any of your favorite television shows, movies and actors. Television shows that are cable classics to you may be shows that she saw back when they were new shows on black-and-white network television before cable television, or even color television, became consumer staples.

While interpersonal attraction is the foundation of any long-term relationship, it is a good idea to inform yourself about the era in which she grew up. You and she will have more to talk about if you make some effort to create common ground. She will appreciate your interest and will give you some brownie points for making the effort to find out a bit more about the sort of things she thinks about and which helped make her into the sort of person she has become.

Older Women And The Human Life Cycle

The human life cycle refers to the different types of predictable things that members of both sexes do at different ages, with different ages corresponding to different stages of the human life cycle. For example, prior to age eighteen, most members of both sexes are usually engaged primarily in educational preparation for later life, and typically depend on their parents for support while so engaged. Sometime during their twenties, most members of both sexes finish their educations, move out of their parents' houses and begin to support themselves. Those who choose to have children typically do so in their twenties and thirties. Few women are biologically capable of conception after age forty. Some women choose to spend a major part of their lives at home raising children during their twenties and thirties, while some others do not.

When women are in their forties and fifties, the children that they had twenty-odd years back have grown old enough to be finishing up school, start become self-supporting and start creating households of their own. Having become accustomed to having their children around for something like twenty years, those women sometimes suffer from empty nest syndrome when their children move out – their home nests have fewer occupants and the women might feel that they have too much unoccupied free time on their hands. Over half of all marriages end in divorce, meaning that if such women should get divorced, they may be the only ones left at home by age forty-five or so.

Divorced women in particular may look back on how they have lived their lives and wish that they had done some things differently – like marry different men than the ones they actually wound up marrying. They may focus on the failings of their ex-husbands in particular, think back to what their ex-husbands were like during their twenties and thirties, think about what the men they wound not marrying were like at that age, mull over all of the little warning signs that they ignored about where their marriages were headed and thereby find themselves quite receptive to male attention from younger men who give them warm feelings. Some may just want boyfriends, and not have the slightest interest in finding new husbands.

Having the advantage of post-divorce twenty/twenty hindsight, they know what types of men to avoid (more specifically, anybody that reminds them of their ex-husbands) they know what types of men best meet whatever needs that such divorced women have figured out actually are their real needs, as opposed to what other people have told them their needs should be (they're not looking for a guy who would be a good father to the kids who have flown the coop, because they're past the stage of needing someone like that) and proceed to take action to reconfigure their lives with the type of man that they should have gotten involved with in the first place (had they only known what they know now). Women have sexual needs, and meeting those needs is at, or very close to, the top of their lists of must-have characteristics for younger men.

Incidentally, dating older women gives you a chance to get involved with types of women you may not have been able to connect with when you were younger. Some women tend to get married younger than other types of women, and people who marry young, when their personalities are still in a state of flux, might wind up growing in different directions than their spouses, and wind up getting divorced due to having become increasingly incompatible with that man who seemed perfect back when both of them were twenty-one. The homecoming queen thus might be back in circulation at thirty-five or forty, and turn out to become a real social possibility for you. Of course, the prom queen at age forty may have evolved into a different sort of person that she was two decades ago.

Different Types Of Older Women

There are as many different types of older women as there are different types of women of other ages. This means that you, as an individual male, will probably appeal to, and be attracted to, some types of older women and have considerably less appeal, and attraction to, to other types of older women. The only way to find out exactly who is your type is to talk with them and thereby allow both of you to learn, and come to conclusions, about each other.

Some older women will be health and fitness fanatics, and will expect younger male companions to share their passions. Some older women will have high powered careers and expect you to fit in with their careers, because they have no intention of changing or dropping their careers to suit you. Some older women will be intellectuals, a few will be anti-intellectuals. They will exhibit the broad spectrum of political opinions found in every age range. There is no single "type."

Some older women will want to have sex twice a day, while others might think once a week is plenty for anybody. Some older women are looking to marry younger men, while others are through with marriage for keeps after having had one (or more) divorces. Some older women will bake you a cake, others will want to dine out almost every night because they hate to cook. Some older women will want to stay at home quite a bit, while others see home as little more than a place to sleep and do the laundry. If you are inclined to look around long enough, you'll find whatever type of older woman it is that you're looking for. Every possible type is out there somewhere waiting for you.

Some types of older women are best avoided. Women of all ages talk a lot about wanting men to respect them, and the same applies to the way they treat you. Older women who don't respect you, in the sense that they disparage you, manipulate you, engage in different sorts of put-downs and assorted other types of disrespectful behavior are women who think little of you. You are free to think as little of such women as they think of you by walking out of their lives whenever you feel like it. It doesn't matter why she acts that way or whether or not it is her fault. You don't have to put up with her problems or waste time on anyone who expects you to put up with it. You don't need to justify your feelings. Many such women will often turn out to be alcoholics, and you don't need to have an alcoholic in your life.

If you don't like the way someone treats you, you can dump her right then and there, regardless of whether she likes it and whether or not you do so in public, whenever you feel like it. Don't waste your time on mean women. You can always do better. Women are fond of saying that they can change their minds any time they want. Men can change their minds about women any time they want and in any setting or circumstances they want, even if women don't like it when men do as they do. You always have unlimited freedom of action.

This also applies to women who are pleasant enough to be with but who ultimately turn out to be incompatible with you. If someone seems nice enough, but you have the feeling that she isn't really right for you, you can exit the relationship any time you want, whether you have met someone you like better or not. Women do this every day, and so should you when you think it is the right thing for you to do. Don't be mean to somebody who is nice to you and seems to means well, but don't waste your time and effort trying to prolong an impossible situation with someone with whom you have no common ground because the two of you are just plain incompatible.

Listen to The Voice Of Your Subconscious

Most of what goes through your mind does so subconsciously, meaning that most of your thought processes are submerged below the threshold of attaining visibility in the conscious parts of the mind. Most of what you think about during the course of a day need not be considered on the conscious level. For example, you wake up each morning, go to the bathroom and proceed to wash and shave while thoughts about what you plan to do at work for the rest of the day fill up ninety-five percent of your stream of consciousness. Washing and shaving are mentally relegated to the periphery of your stream of consciousness, because you have chosen to relegate them to that status, either consciously or by default.

Once you have consciously decided that something is right for you and worthy of your immediate attention, deciding that something should be so sets up a sort of alert system in the subconscious part of the mind. This subconscious alert system signals the conscious part of the mind, meaning the part of the mind where you take care of things in the here-and-now part of life, when something noteworthy comes into view in the external world, or when the subconscious mind notes or detects a pattern, relationship or correlation that is worthy of your conscious attention.

Listen to the voice of your subconscious mind both when seeking an older woman and while you are involved with her. If you keep having thoughts that a relationship that you are in is not an ideal situation for you, move on.

Why Some Younger Men Should Not Date Older Women

Certain types of younger men are unlikely to be compatible or successful with older women. Younger men who can't stop behaving and dressing as if they were dating someone their own age are unclear on the concept that they must modify their behavior when socializing with different types of people such as older women, and such younger men will find the going tough with older women until such time as they change their ways. A twenty year old man cannot talk with a woman who is forty-five years old, meaning somebody who is in his mother's age range, in the same way he talks with a woman who is twenty years old, meaning somebody who is in his sister's age range. Such a younger man is unclear on the concept that she has had different sorts of life experiences that he has had, and expects different things of him because she has had those life experiences.

The most serious problem of all is the younger man's underlying mindset. You might not know as much as you should about how to talk with a woman who is ten or twenty years older than you are as regards an ongoing male-female relationship, but at the very least you should talk to her respectfully and in complete sentences. Talking in disrespectful monosyllables is not the way to turn on older women. If you want to spend time in a relationship, take the time to act as if you are an adult and are interested in working at making the relationship work. That means talking and acting in an adult manner when in close proximity with an adult female.

Younger men who want to have children of their own or are seeking public approval of their relationships should not enter into relationships with older women. After age forty, women are rarely able to have children. A man who wants children would be best off with either a younger woman, or consider the adoption option.

Finally, some men can't handle public social disapproval that a relationship between an older woman and a younger man will inevitably attract, and such men should steer clear of dating older women. Men who can't handle public disapproval are unlikely candidates for age-discrepant relationships, which will inevitably attract potshots from the general public.

CHAPTER THREE
How To Pick Up
Older Women

Preparing To Pick Up Older Women

When you're looking to meet older women, doing certain things improves your ability to make initial contact and maintain initial contact.

Take a bath every day, even on weekends when your job does not require you to be clean. The female sense of smell is somewhat more acute than the male sense of smell, and older women will make on-the-spot negative judgments about you if you attempt to initiate a conversation with older women while on line at a supermarket or after church services when body odors of the sort usually confined to a gym locker start wafting their way from you to their delicate little noses. Don't try to cover up your body odor with cologne. Do take a bath or shower every day before going outside, and scrub every inch of your skin clean. Scrub your ears out as well. Shampoo your hair and comb it. Clean the dirt out from under your fingernails and then clip those fingernails as well. Last but not least, brush your teeth before you go outside. Few things are more repulsive to a woman than talking with a man whose smile has a protective coating of dental plaque. The lack of personal cleanliness will be automatically interpreted by women of all ages as the twin cousin of unhealthiness. You may think that these preparatory steps are unnecessary, but you never know when someone interesting might cross paths with you when you just happen to be walking two blocks to pick up something to eat. Cleanliness counts.

The female sense of smell, also known as the olfactory sense, is important for another reason. The sense of smell is linked to the brain's limbic system, which controls emotions. Being clean both clears away old, unpleasant smells from your body and allows fresh male sweat, known as axillary secretions, to enter the air around you and drift towards women near you. The smell of male sweat is known to improve female mood, reduce tension and increase relaxation, most likely through effects on the female neuroendocrine system. Smelling clean thus helps create a positive initial emotional impression in older women. (Bhutta, Preti)

Wear clean clothing devoid of tears, patches and other obvious flaws and irregularities. On the other hand, don't dress up like you are a sophisticated world traveler if you are not. Dress like other young men your age, but avoid wearing anything that plays up some characteristic that is narrowly specific to men in your age group, such as music groups that women ten years older than you have never heard of. Taking the opposite approach can sometimes help you get a conversation going or even encourage an older woman to initiate a conversation with you. Taking the opposite approach means wearing a shirt with the logo or name of a music group ten or more years older than the groups with which the people in your age range are familiar, such as a concert tour t-shirt specific to a group that older women knew way back when that group was either unknown or up-and-coming. Just be sure that you know a few of their songs and some odd facts about them if you want to be able to conduct a meaningful introductory conversation about that musical group. The way you dress counts.

The majority of older women you are likely to meet have probably been married at some point in time, and are also likely to have been divorced or widowed. The implication is that they have lived with men for many years, and are used to eye contact as a daily part of their everyday lives. They will not act like little girls who are afraid that boys will catch them looking at them. If you try to pick up an older woman and you are not good at eye contact, they are unlikely to become interested in you. Older women may be interested in younger men in general, but are not interested in younger men who act excessively younger than they actually are, psychologically speaking. They are looking for younger men who know the basics of acting something like a real adult male who just happens to be at the lower end of the age scale. Older women will not expect you to be as smooth and sophisticated as men their own age, but they will expect you to know the alphabet of behaving like an adult.

Adult males should be good at making and maintaining direct eye contact with adult females, older and younger. Women enjoy eye contact, and younger men who are good at eye contact will do well with older women, assuming, of course that they have several other things going for them, like a good personality and physical health. Men who are not good at making eye contact will not do as well with women. Women do not like men who cannot make eye contact. Incidentally, when women are interested in men, their pupils dilate, and men consider this an attractive trait in women. (Porter)

Smile at older women. Women of all ages usually take it as a compliment, even if they are not interested in taking you up on your implied offer to initiate a conversation and possibly even a relationship.

Smiling at an older woman is one way of telling her that you are interested in her as a romantic possibility. Smiling is a form of nonverbal communication with a strong emotional component, because it is intended to communicate an emotional reaction, or intention, to another person.

Smiles work best in conjunction with simultaneous eye contact. Smile while looking at your intended romantic possibility. In addition, move your body a bit closer towards any older woman you are talking with and oriented in her direction. Feel free to make a few gestures while talking with her to show that you are animated, and not an all-talk-and-no-action sort of guy. Smiling counts. (Otta)

Your Appearance Counts

Everybody judges everybody else to some degree based on their appearance. Older women will use your appearance as a basis for evaluating you with respect to whether or not they will consider getting involved with you. Women of all ages do this, and older women are no exception to this rule. You do the same when you evaluate an older woman's attractiveness. Men in general make a decision to make a move on, or not make a move on, an older woman in part based on her appearance, and the quality that underlies her overall physical appearance is her health. No matter how great a figure a woman might have, if she looks unhealthy, you will probably back off from all thoughts of approaching her or seeking to get involved with her.

The first thing that younger men who are looking to meet, and get involved with, older women need to do is to take care of their overall health and appearance. If you do not look healthy, you will not look like a candidate for a mutually healthy relationship.

First of all, get eight hours of sleep a night every night. It may sound like fun to be a workaholic who gets by on five hours of sleep a night, but your brain and body don't see sleep deprivation as any sort of laughing matter. The more sleep you miss out on a regular basis, the greater the extent to which a broad array of your cognitive and bodily functions will become impaired, ineffective and depressed. Sleep deprivation makes you both look physically unhealthy and run-down as well as sound psychologically dimwitted. People who don't get enough sleep also tend to have more accidents than people who do get enough sleep, because they are less fully aware of what is going on around them and what they are doing. Not too many women, older or younger, want to get involved, let alone get into bed, with a man who sounds like he's not all there because he does not get enough sleep. (Van Dongen)

Get eight or more hours of sleep on a regular basis and you will both look physically healthier and speak with greater mental functionality than when you fail to get enough sleep. Sleep deprivation reduces and depresses sexual functioning along with various other cognitive and bodily functions. Incidentally, sleep deprivation will also make you unnecessarily hungry when you have had plenty of to eat already and make you gain weight for no good reason, because sleep insufficiency disrupts the human hormonal equilibrium that regulates hunger.

The end result is that not getting enough sleep makes you gain weight, because not getting enough sleep will keep you hungry all day and night long, and make you eat to excess when you really do not need to eat at all. (Spiegel)

Second, lay off the alcohol and tobacco. There are no health benefits whatsoever to be gained from consuming alcohol and tobacco. Alcohol is medically classified as a central nervous system depressant. Consuming alcohol produces hangovers as a result of encouraging various biochemical waste products to build up in the brain and the body. Alcohol consumption also depresses sexual functioning. Last, but not least, alcohol impairs your social skills and your verbal abilities. You might think that you are a social maestro when you are intoxicated, but you will be the one and only person in the world that thinks so. Smoking tobacco produces lung cancer and other health problems. Particles of tobacco smoke take up residence in the lungs, block the ability to take in oxygen and reduce sexual functioning by limiting the amount of oxygen that the body can take in.

Change your diet to a healthy diet if you are not already following one. This will improve your health, appearance and sexual functioning. Eat fruits, vegetables, lean meat, whole grains and some low-fat dairy products. Lay off the sugar, pasta, potatoes, sauces, burgers and fries. If you work at a desk, you do not need to consume more than about two thousand calories a day, because you do not exert yourself at a desk enough to burn off more than two thousand calories a day.

Clothing that is acceptable among people your own age is less acceptable among older women. If you habitually wear clothing featuring the names of your favorite musical groups, advertising slogans, web sites and so on, you will simply look juvenile to older women, and looking juvenile means that they will steer clear of you, because you are not providing them with any visible evidence that you are capable of interacting with them on an adult level. If you want to meet older women, leave your age-specific clothing at home. Wear the sort of clothing that you would wear if you were out shopping for a business suit – subdued and not identifiably age-specific. You don't have to look like you work as an accountant, but you should look like you are ready to interact with your mother's best friend, meaning that you should leave the sort of clothing that is suitable only for socializing with people in your own age range at home.

Again, the most important thing about appearance is to appear to be in good health. Good health, or at least the appearance of good health, makes you sexually appealing by virtue of advertising-by-implication that you are physically fit, energetic and possibly open to a mutually enjoyable sexual relationship. To be blunt, if you do not look healthy, you might not look like you are capable of satisfying an older woman's sexual desires. Make no mistake about it, if you do not look like you are potentially capable of vigorous sex, you are probably out of the running for a relationship with an older woman.

While not all older men are sexually dysfunctional, men who have spent a couples of decades at desk jobs have often gained too much weight, and lost too much heart function, to even walk up a flight of stairs without sweating, and have pasty, unhealthy-looking skin and muscle tone, which is why such men are not eagerly sought out by women of any age. If older women slot you into this category, you are in trouble.

You need not look like a professional bodybuilder or athlete to look healthy. You need not work out in a gym, but do need to have some muscles on your body, so get some light exercise on a regular basis, preferably every day. Try walking for an hour a day to develop your leg muscles and improve your heart-lung action. Flabby muscles are not sexy.

Pickups

Pickups are forms of social interaction where one party attempts to initiate a conversation with member of the opposite sex and develop that in initial conversation into an ongoing conversation for the purpose of initiating a short-term or long-term relationship. Either a man or a woman can initiate a pickup. Pickups can involve total strangers or casual acquaintances, such as the sort of people who see each other now and then getting off the same train station without ever having had a conversation.

Salesmen practice sales presentations, also known as sales pitches, to help them sell products and services. While you do not need to have an hour-long monologue presentation prepared to initiate a conversation with someone, it is a good idea to have a few canned pickup lines of your own that happen to mesh well with your personality, as well as a few canned responses to pickup lines initiated by older women. It is important to be cognizant that you could bump into an opportunity at any random moment and thus need to have some verbiage ready to roll when opportunity knocks on your door.

If you see an older woman standing on the street looking around as if she is lost, ask her if she is lost or a newcomer looking a particular place. You can even walk her there to wherever it is that she wants to go while seeing if a conversation develops or to find out whether she is inclined to volunteer contact information.

If you see an older woman somewhere in the supermarket who looks interesting, walk over to her and ask something about what she thinks of whatever sort of merchandise it is that she is browsing.

If you go to a church regularly, take note of the ladies who go there and move closer to someone that you consider interesting with each passing week. Ask something about the church, what she is wearing or anything else you want after services are over.

Before trying to pick up anyone, be sure to determine whether or not she is wearing a wedding ring.

An older woman can try to pick you up, of course, meaning ask you where place is even though she knows quite well exactly where it is, since this is a way to get a conversation going with an interesting-looking younger man.

Now and then during the course of your life you will be walking down the street and find someone catching your eye, while becoming aware that you are simultaneously catching her eye as well. These situations are great opportunities. When you get within a few feet of such a woman, slowly come to a stop, give a little smile and say something, anything, such as I don't think that I've seen you around here before or I don't think that I know who you are. If she stops walking, keep the conversation moving along, say anything at all, just don't let the pace of conversation come to a crashingly complete and silent stop. She might even do her best to help you keep it moving along if she wants to help you keep talking to her. Keep in mind that a woman ten to twenty years older than you has had a lot of guys make moves on her over the course of the many years before you strolled into her life, so she has some idea of how to respond to your conversational attempts, assuming that she is interested in you. If she is not interested she will keep walking.

Older women who want to get picked up will dress in ways carefully calculated to get male attention. Personal ads consist of salesmanship in print, while the way a woman dresses consists of salewomanship in cloth. Clothing designed to show off her figure is always a dead giveaway that she is looking for a guy. High heels, low-cut dresses and certain other articles of fashion are specifically designed, and purchased, by women to attract men by capturing their attention. You can be sure of one thing: women do not dress up that way when they are alone at home without male audiences to notice them, and they expend considerable time and effort getting themselves ready to get noticed by guys like you. If you like the way an older woman is dressed, say so, because she probably spent a bit of time that day getting ready to get noticed – by you. Women don't like to get all dressed up with nobody to go out with while so attired.

Sometimes older women will initiate "probing" semi-pickup conversations with a younger man to see if he has anything at all going on upstairs as well as to help her probe for potential mutual interest. If an older woman asks a younger man standing in line at the supermarket about a particular new product she sees him bringing to the checkout register, his response allows her to see whether or not he can think on his feet and thereby judge whether his thought processes can be categorized in the acceptable zone of the adult range. A younger man who both explains a new product to an older woman in comprehensible language and tells her that the new type of fat-free ice cream that he is in the process of buying just happens to also be available at the ice cream store with tables where the two of them can sit down a block away from the food store that they are both chatting away in, that sort of younger man may be just the sort of younger man that she is looking for.

If an older woman at a copy shop asks you for a suggestion on how to enlarge or shrink something, a question that she could just as easily ask someone who works in that copy shop, explain as best as you can and offer to help her with whatever copying job it is that she is trying to get done, while being sure to tell her a bit about yourself and ask a few questions. If she likes you, she'll open up conversationally.

If an older woman keeps looking at you on the street, in a restaurant, in a church or some other social context, wave at her, say hello or whatever else works for you, and then walk over to her and start talking with her about anything you want.

Get A Dialogue Going

When you approach an older woman, or when an older woman approaches you, the only way that you are going to be able to leverage that initial contact into some sort of ongoing relationship, be it short-term or long-term, is to get some sort of dialogue going and keep it going. A dialogue is a conversation where the things each of you talk about acknowledges what the other is talking about, and each of you adjusts what you say next in response to what the other person just said.

A dialogue is not a monologue where you would simply give a woman the same prepared speech that you would give to any other woman. A dialogue similarly does not consist of two people taking turns delivering their own monologues without any degree of acknowledgement of what the other is saying. Two alternating monologues do not add up into a dialogue. If she says that she has a pet dog, the very next thing you say is that you used to have a dog that was of a certain type, but the new place you live in is too small to accommodate a dog of any type. If she says that she is divorced, you say next that you

70

are single. Whatever she says, tie in whatever you say next to whatever it is that she just said, because that fact that you are doing so tells her that you are listening and paying attention on some level to what she is saying. Women like it when men pay attention to them.

Conducting a worthwhile dialogue requires that you say things about yourself that reveal characteristics that might be of specific interest to an older woman. For example, if you try to pick up an older woman while standing in line at a supermarket, ask her about how the fruit, spaghetti sauce, ice cream or whatever it is that you see her buying is. If she gives any sort of reply beyond a monosyllabic grunt, tell her a bit about your own (slightly different tastes) in ice cream or whatever and see how she responds. If she says something, acknowledge it and use it as a starting point for the next thing you say.

Mention anything that reveals something about you. Maybe you avoid eating chicken skins because there's too much fat in them. Maybe you eat a lot of fruit because you like eating fruit after you exercise. Mention something along the lines of how your ex-girlfriend liked to eat something, this will tip her off that you are single and looking. In the course of a pickup conversation, it is okay to mention that you have male roommates, because that lets her know that you are not married. If she mentions anything about her marital status or ex-husband, such as having gotten divorced three years ago, find some sort of way to stay in contact with her, either then and there, or later on – by telephone, e-mail or whatever. Maybe offer to carry her groceries.

If she mentions her age under any sort of pretext, even if it does not fit in with whatever other things she is talking about, she is interested in you and wants to see how you react to hearing her mention her age. Always make eye contact with any woman who says this with at least a hint of a smile on your face and say something in a relaxed-and-enjoying-yourself sort of tone of voice, okay, I'm (state your age) and single. At that point you can either suggest that the two of you drop into the nearest coffeehouse, ice cream store, pizza joint or whatever it is that is closest to where you are at the moment, because you want to capitalize on her receptive mood while it is still fresh in her mind by continuing the conversation in an uninterrupted manner. If that is not possible, exchange telephone numbers or other contact information, and hold the door open for her as the two of you exit the store. You can also offer to help her with her groceries. If you meet someone at night, settle for contact information rather than trying to persuade her to walk down a dark street with you.

If an older woman with whom you are chatting starts laughing, gesturing with her hands and so on, she is interested in you and you need to do something as soon as possible to lock in her interest.

In the course of any conversation that you are able to going, be sure to mention exactly what it is that you do for a living. Get that information out to her in the first fifteen minutes or so that the two of you are talking – bartender, accountant, college student, cook or whatever else it is that you do. If you wish, mention the name of whatever company you work for and maybe tell a few very short stories about the company's activities, products or the people you work with, just to reinforce the impression that you are part of the adult workaday world.

If an older woman suggests something on her own initiative during the course of a conversation such as talking with her at some future date over coffee, she is interested in you. If your circumstances at the moment allow you to do so, suggest that the two of you visit a coffeehouse immediately. It is not the specific place, or kind of place, that the two of you go to that matters so much as taking advantage of a good moment to have an extended conversation when the two of you are presumably feeling a bit light-headed upon having met each other. Lock in her interest and good feelings while they are still fresh in the mind.

Whatever you do during an initial dialogue, don't harp or dwell on anything negative, even if it is something that is fresh in your mind or something you feel an inexplicable need to dwell on. Don't mention a disagreement with your landlord, the job you got fired from, a relative you dislike, or anything else that might distract her from realizing what a wonderful guy you are to spend time with. Salesmen don't sell products by harping on negative characteristics of those products. Negatives don't sell.

People will look at, and keep looking at, the two of you when you and she sit down in a restaurant or coffeehouse. Ignore them and focus your attention and gaze on her. Tune into the lady you are with, not the peanut gallery. Hold the door for her and pull the chair out for her. If the two of you are enjoying yourselves, you should be conscious of what is going on between you and her and not much of anything else.

One thing that women like to have men volunteer during an initial conversation is what men are looking for in a relationship. If you are looking for a casual relationship, marriage or anything in between, tell her so. If you are not sure what you are looking for, it is always acceptable to say that you are looking for someone who is friendly and compatible, and you want to see what might develop from that point. Even if you are not inclined to marry someone older than you are, don't blurt out that sort of thing during an initial conversational encounter. You might change your mind, she might have a girlfriend who is just right for you, and you do not want to focus on anything that she might perceive as negative, even if you think it makes perfect sense to you to talk about it. Negatives don't sell.

Women who have been around longer than you know that relationships involve a lot of fumbling around on the part of both parties, and many people don't know what they are looking for until after they get. Even worse, some men don't realize how good they had it until after they lose it, so don't limit your options too early in the game. Keep your options open.

If she brings up the subject of age as a general discussion topic, just mention that you do not see how an age difference would present a problem for you, even if some other people see it differently. If she asks you why it is not a problem for you, say that it is a purely individual-chemistry sort of thing, and that individuals have to work it out between themselves, but do not need to work it out with the rest of the world. Then ask her if she sees some specific thing about an age difference that raises questions in her mind. It might be a new idea for her, and she may not know what to do or say next, since having a relationship with a younger man might not be a subject she has spent a lot of time dwelling on.

How To Tell If She's Interested In You

Before you start talking with a particular older woman, the most common way to tell that she finds you attractive is that she looks at you with at least a hint of smile on her face. This means that she is at least open to the possibility of a noncommittal introductory chat with you to see if her initial attraction might develop into a real sense of burgeoning interest in you. If someone smiles at you, looks at you, waves at you, turns in your direction or some combination of those actions, you are on safe ground making a move on her.

You can talk about anything you want with an older woman who has gone out of her way to notice you, the subject is completely irrelevant, if she is attracted to you on some level. Just don't make yourself out to be an idiot by making a sexual proposition the first time you talk with her. Don't use any of the contemporary slang of your age group, she won't understand what the slang means, and lack of understanding is a barrier to the sort of communication that an exciting relationship requires. Be sure to smile at her, look at her and turn your body in her direction.

After the two of you have been talking for fifteen minutes or so, watch and see whether her behavior towards you changes in any way. The first sign that she likes you is the extent to which she laughs for no discernible reason except that she happens to be talking with you, gestures with her hands, turns her body around a bit, her eyes crinkle up and generally acts happy because she is with you. She may even be getting a bit aroused by being around you. If an older woman acts like this, you are on the inside track with her and you need to continue talking with her then and there.

You also need to either let her know that you are interested in either moving the conversation the two of you have going to a place where the two of you can sit down, such as the nearest possible coffee shop or pizzeria. The next best thing to do is for the two of you to exchange contact information so that the two of you can meet in the next few days, maybe after the two of you have chatted a bit over the phone. Be sure to call her either later that day or the very next day. Better to sound a shade too enthusiastic instead of appearing to be playing hard to get. Playing hard to get, or pretending to be disinterested, will work against you. A woman who is older than you knows it to be an adolescent game and will categorize you as being too adolescent to have a relationship with an adult woman.

When an older woman seems to be enthusiastic about you, show that you share her enthusiasm. Smile at her, look at her, turn your body in her direction, laugh at appropriate moments and, no matter what else happens, do your part to keep the conversational dialogue going. Nobody can remain conversationally deep forever, but the purpose of keeping the conversation going at that point is to make and maintain contact with her by maintaining the good-feelings state of mind.

Women practice selling men on the idea that it is a good idea for men to spend time with them. They give men reasons to initiate conversations with women. They don't call it salesmanship (salewomanship?), but that is what they actually do. A salesman dresses up in a suit to make the sale, and that is what women do when they set out to meet men – they dress up and they sell men on the idea that they are nice ladies for men to spend time with. A salesman delivers a sales pitch, whereas women laugh, giggle, gesture (and maybe even talk somewhere along the line) as part of making their sales pitch to men. Making men feel good about talking with women gives the men a reason to want to get relationships going. A salesman closes the sales when both parties agree to do something that they both want to do, such as buying a product as a result of seeing certain things eye-to-eye.

This is what women do when they try to get a relationship going with a man. Closing a sale means that the salesman has been able to communicate, and to thereby transfer, the enthusiasm in his mind to the mind of the sales prospect. Sounds a lot like what happens with a budding romance, doesn't it?

Not all older women will be giggling with enthusiasm within fifteen minutes of first meeting you. They may have some degree of initial interest in you, but will play their cards closer to the vest until they find out more about you. They will just talk with you in an open-minded, but noncommittal, fashion, and it is up to you to keep the conversation going. Talk calmly, but don't talk so slowly and unenthusiastically that they conclude that you are just going through the motions of being interested.

Talk with the sort of enthusiasm that you reserve for somebody that you are interested in, but don't start whooping it up until after she starts to show some home-grown enthusiasm. If she volunteers some information that might allow you to maintain future contact with her, such as a work telephone number, always jot it down and give her your corresponding contact information.

If an older woman volunteers any sort of contact information about her relationship, status, something along the lines of having gotten divorced six weeks ago, you can be sure that she is inviting a response from you to see what your relationship status is as well as to see what you will suggest to her about staying in contact with you. For example, if she says that she got divorced six weeks ago, you should reply that since you broke up with someone a few months ago, you are back in the singles scene – say anything that moves the conversation along and encourages her to do her part to keep the conversation moving along and encourage further contact.

If she volunteers her age directly, or goes through verbal somersaults to indirectly let you know how long ago it was that she finished high school and got divorced a year ago, she is probing you to see what you think of her age. Do not say anything critical or negative that might turn her off. Above all, do not ask anything along the lines of whether she has trouble meeting men in her own age range. Do not mention the general subject of men in her own age range for any reason until she brings it up. After age thirty or so, the ranks of single men thin out, and women know it, so don't harp on what is probably an anxiety-engendering topic for her. Talk about you and her, not the state of the singles marketplace in general.

Again, when she mentions her age, directly or indirectly, just say, that's nice, I'm (state your age) and move on conversationally. Most preferably, you move on to a conversation topic that directly or indirectly brings up the topic of the two of you socializing further down the line. Tell her words to the effect that you'd like to talk further with her and suggest that the two of you sit down in at the nearest coffeehouse or whatever. When you get there, or maybe along the way, tell her that you are into jogging, and ask if jogging is something that she is into as well. If she is not into jogging, tell her that she is invited to join you when you go jogging in a public place the next time you engage in that activity. Incidentally, jogging is a sport that also allows you to wear less clothing than usual in public, and she might turn out to have a thing for something about your physique once she sees your body in action.

Writing A Personal Ad To Meet An Older Woman

Advertising is widely used by both organizations and people to inform their target audiences about what they have to offer and to invite interested parties to make contact for detailed information. Companies advertise to generate leads for salesmen. That may sound very cut-and-dried, but that is what life is all about. You have to promote yourself to other people. If older women do not know that you exist, you might as well be on a desert island by yourself. You can attempt to meet older women either in person or through intermediating media using personal ads.

If something about the way you communicate in person, or what you are communicating through a personal ad, fails to communicate the key proposition that you are interested and available for a relationship with certain types of compatible older women, you might as well be on a desert island by yourself. Give them a reason to want to make contact with you by saying something about yourself that will entice them.

Good advertising consists of salesmanship in print and nothing more, though it can be supplemented with other sorts of information, such as pictures. A personal advertisement is no exception to this rule. It has no other purpose beyond letting a target audience of older female prospects for relationships with younger men know that you are trying to establish a relationship with an interested and compatible older woman and that you are inviting a response to your advertisement. Relationships are no different than other areas of life in the sense that you have to sell yourself to other people or groups of people (such as college admissions offices), either in person or through intermediaries such as media. You have to tell people that you exist, you have to tell them what you have to offer and you have to give them a reason to respond to your advertisement by telling them what's in it for them if they should decide to contact you. This presupposes that you know something about what older women are like, know what sort of incentives would interest them and use what you know about them as a basis for appealing to them using salesmanship in print in a personal ad. (Lord and Thomas)

For example, although you studied in high school to get good grades, getting into college required that you actually communicate directly with the college admissions department and sell them on the idea of taking you in as a student. You can't expect the colleges to go to the trouble of trying to find out that you exist. You used your grades and test scores and admission application to conduct this particular selling job. If you did not fill out an application, your failure to directly communicate your interest to the college in that manner would mean that you would not get to establish a relationship with that college as a student.

You must sell yourself directly to that college, and your grades and test scores were your major selling points that gave them reason to want to admit you as a student (unless you happened to be an athlete).

What is considered a great selling point with one audience might be considered neutral or negative with another audience. Your buddies in high school may have chosen to associate with you because you were able to talk on a meaningful level (meaningful to them, that is) about sports, movies, television shows and musical groups. Bringing up those same selling points in the course of applying for admission to college would be worse than useless, because colleges have no interest in the things that your buddies in high school hold in high regard. Similarly, things that males and females in your own age range hold in high regard might not be considered good selling points when considered by older women with different priorities. Understand your audience when writing a personal ad.

Although you may not be particularly interested in writing and running a personal ad, writing one can help you clarify and fine-tune the image that you want to present to older women as well as clarify and fine-tune exactly what it is you are looking for in an older woman. Getting it in writing forces you to think about what you are doing and what you are looking for, and you could use it as a rough draft for what you say when you meet older women one-on-one. This assumes, of course that you are acting on the basis of information about older women, in the sense that you actually know something about them. (Lord and Thomas)

The more real information you offer about yourself and what you are looking for, the better the chances that your personal ad will attract the sort of older women that you are looking for. Presenting information about yourself will be seen by some of the older women who read your personal ad as a reason to respond to it. The less real information that you provide about yourself and what you are looking for in an older woman, the worse your personal ad will read and the less likely it is that it will attract anybody at all, let alone anybody compatible, because they will have little or no idea what you offer to them and what you are looking for in an older woman.

For example, writing a vague personal ad that states that you are a hot younger guy looking for an exciting older lady says almost nothing about you, your age, your background and what sort of characteristics you are looking for in a female companion. If you talk like that in person, don't expect anything good to happen. Offering real information about yourself counts.

An effective personal ad communicates key selling points that would be of interest to older women, while also communicating what you are seeking as far as compatibility goes. Salesmanship in print includes communicating what your limitations might be, or at least limitations that might be of interest to older women. For example, if you are twenty-five years old, a young lady close to your own age might not care whether or not you live in your parents' basement, but a lady ten to twenty years older might see that as a negative. Spell out your limitations concisely and truthfully. Don't waste other people's time.

Personal ads should always include a physical description and background demographic information about you. Always include your age so that the different types of older women who prefer younger men in different age ranges can evaluate you. Different older women have different ideas about how much younger a younger man that's right for them "should" be. If you are twenty-five, some thirty-five year olds might see you as "too young" for them, while some forty-five year olds might think that a twenty-five year old is "perfect" for them. Different people see things differently, so don't generalize and don't have any preconceptions. (Bytheway)

Always include your height. A lot of women, older and younger, will not date anyone shorter then themselves. If you read through personal ads published almost anywhere, you will see that a lot of women have a height preference. Interestingly enough, you will find that women of below-average height seem to be compelled to seek out men of above-average height. Opposites attract, or at least some people seem to wish that they did.

Be sure to mention your body type – thin, average, athletic or heavyset, or whatever type you happen to be. It is not required, but it is a good idea to include your hair color and eye color. Some women have a fixation on a particular hair or eye color, just as you might have a fixation on women of a particular age range or body type.

If you have a job, be sure to mention that you are either "employed" or are an engineer, laborer, or whatever it is that you do. Older women who got divorced from husbands who were unemployed for extended periods of time are often leery of getting involved with younger men, presumably in good health, who don't work for a living. (South)

State your location. Older women want to know how close you are to their home base. Few are interested in long-distance relationships, though some might respond to men who state that they are "open to relocation," assuming that you actually are open to that possibility.

Your personality is superimportant to women in general and older women in particular. If they don't like your personality, don't expect anything interesting to happen. Use words that people who have actually known you have used to describe you: "nice guy," "honest," "sense of humor," "open-minded," "romantic" and other positive words. If you misrepresent yourself, you will be found out to have misrepresented yourself within fifteen minutes of an initial one-on-one conversation, so be particularly careful about the wording of your personality self-description. Do not describe yourself as "mature" unless numerous other people have described you that way. Keep in mind that what sounds mature to friends your own age might not sound very mature to someone ten years older than you.

Some people like to include a few words about their beliefs and activities: "great cook," "I like camping," "football enthusiast," "Christian," "dog lover" and so on. This is strictly optional, but if you enjoy and seek out certain activities, that says something about you, and mentioning what you do in your spare time might reel in a fellow enthusiast.

Mention briefly what you are looking for with respect to a new relationship: casual dating, an affair, a long-term relationship or whatever else it is that you have in mind.

Spell out exactly what you are looking for in an older woman. This means spelling out either what age bracket you consider acceptable (thirties, forties, fifties, sixties, or just state a numerical age range). This means spelling out what sort of personality type you are looking for ("nice lady," "workaholic," "laid back," sports enthusiast") and so on. If you are looking for a particular physical type of some sort, spell it out: "over six feet tall;" "busty;" "blonde" and so on.

Spell out what you are looking for as far as her family situation: does she have kids at home? Divorced women over forty-five are less likely to have kids at home, women under forty more so.

Some older women are completely uninhibited about dating younger men who might be younger than their sons, and some such women may have sons older than you living at home with them. Maybe you can deal with this, maybe not. Maybe they can deal with this, maybe not (if they live in mom's house, they had better get used to adjusting to mom's lifestyle and that fact that mom has sexual needs). If you can deal with this, state: "kids at home okay." If you can't, state: "no kids at home, please." If you have kids of your own, be absolutely sure to mention that fact in your self-description.

If you have any sort of disability or health problem, such as diabetes, be sure to state exactly what it is: "diabetic." Women who have the same disability or health problem as you are out there, by the way.

After you write your personal ad, put it way for a few days, or maybe even for a few weeks. Sleep on it. Look it over with a fresh mind later on and try to read it from the point of view of an older woman reading it for the first time. If it doesn't read crisply and clearly, or seems confusing, rewrite it until it is easier to read and easy to figure out what it is that you are trying to communicate. Measure and monitor your responses after you actually run your ad. Are there trends?

Do women in a certain part of the age range you specified, certain locations or some other slant, trend or dimension that you did not expect, seem to predominate in the responses you get?

CHAPTER FOUR
Getting Past
Public Opinion

The Hardest Thing About
Dating Older Women

For many younger men, the hardest thing about dating older women is dealing with the general public's occasional pointing, staring, snickering, whispering, giggling and occasional outright public comments about age-discrepant relationships that they happen to be in. The way that the world works is that when you go out in public, some people will react to seeing you in a relationship with a visibly older woman by exhibiting these sorts of reactions. Some younger men can readily disregard these sorts of public reactions right from the start in a relationship with older women, while others have to acclimate themselves to learning how to disregard such behavior.

Older women have probably either seen other older women get into relationships with younger men, or have taken the time to give some thought to how they might deal with public reaction to being seen involved with a younger man. What they have given thought to is not so much resolving what it is that they want but rather how to get around, push back against and ignore other people's reactions to seeing them going after, and getting involved with, younger men. Some older women are more sensitive to this than others.

Younger men tend to have an easier time of it, if only because their peers are most often either neutral or mildly, if humorously, supportive of a younger man who gets involved with an older woman. Men under the age of forty are most likely to be mildly supportive, or at least avoid being anti-supportive. After age forty, attitudes change somewhat, though most men still tend to remain neutral about the issue of younger men dating older women, except in cases where it involves a woman known to them personally, such as their mother.

The more physically unhealthy a man becomes after age forty, the less likely he is to be supportive of older women getting involved with younger men because he may have a subconscious neurotic fear that he is no longer the hottest guy in town after sitting at a desk for twenty plus years. At the end of the line, this is really a form of sexual neurosis. A man who becomes restless about seeing two people sauntering down the street where the woman happens to be substantially older than the male member of the couple is actually revealing that his mind is riddled with thoughts of neurotic sexual insecurity and how he thinks that he fails to measure up against younger, and possibly physically healthier, competition for women.

There are men out there who think like this, and both they and their opinions (if they get to the point of stating them in your presence) are no more than houseflies to be brushed off. As long as you consider their opinions irrelevant, they will remain irrelevant. When you make the mistake of regarding their opinions as anything more than symptoms of neurosis, that is where you start creating problems for yourself. Other people's opinions about your relationship don't count, and the opinions of neurotics count for even less.

Women generally think about relationships more than men, and are thus ready at the drop of a hat to come out with an opinion about any woman involved in any sort of supposed sexual relationship with a man substantially younger than herself. The more neurotic the woman, the more livid her expressed disapproval of age-discrepant relationships will be. A divorced woman over forty who has had no luck finding a man after her divorce will have no inhibitions whatsoever about giving voice to her dissatisfaction with the way her life has turned out when she sees another woman walking down the street with a new guy who happens to be substantially younger. When she sees another woman having what she does not have herself, possibly because she has self-imposed mental barriers against pursuing younger men, her neurotic sexual dissatisfaction will take on an animated and highly disparaging verbal form. When people see other people enjoying what they literally cannot get their hands on themselves, they often become frustrated and even angry.

Neurotic people do not think rationally. A feverish jumble of irrational emotions thrash around within their minds. Neurotic irrationality includes dredging up irrationally irrelevant issues that in fact do not have any logical significance as regards to older women dating younger men, and they go out of their way to pretend that such irrelevancies are true when in fact they have no basis in reality whatsoever.

The two most common irrational irrelevancies that neurotics bring up when dwelling on age-discrepant relationships are: "she's old enough to be his mother" and "he's young enough to be her son." These phrases usually pop up in emotionally charged conversations with undisguised undertones of disapproval. The reason that neurotics dwell on age-discrepant relationships in this manner is that their feverishly disorganized minds are trying to project the incest taboo onto older woman-younger man relationships, even when it does not fit the facts of adult age-discrepant relationships in any way. (Vera, Berardo and Berardo) The incest taboo on sexual relationships between sexual relationships between members of the same family is a near-universal taboo found in almost all cultures, but this taboo applies only to members of the same family, meaning blood relatives. The incest taboo does not apply to adult non-relatives who happen to be of different ages and who happen to like being with each other.

If a child or a neurotic once had a problem with a person with red hair, it might later turn out that the neurotic would over-generalize their experiences and thereafter irrationally avoid anyone with red hair. Any person or object, such as a painting of someone with red hair, that happened to exhibit that single characteristic would become an object of fear, despite the irrationality of that fear. Neurotics can't think straight, so they think in this sort of warped manner and tell the world about it.

The same principle applies to neurotics who mistakenly confuse relationships characterized by age difference with incestuous mother-son relationships, even when the adults in such relationships are not relatives. The fact of the matter is that relationships that happen to include people with age differences does not logically signify anything at all beyond irrationally neurotic thought processes in the minds of those who see what is not there. Since neurotics do not know what they are talking about, there is no need to pay attention to them when they use illegitimate characterizations in an attempt to stigmatize you. If you do not accept their attempts at stigmatization, stigmatization will not take root in your mind. (Goffman).

When people say bizarre things to the effect that think younger men dating older women is unnatural or disgusting, you are free to publicly point out that they are completely in error, and that the truth of the matter is that they are guilty of irrationally and illogically confusing a legitimate older woman – younger man relationship with incest. Adults, children and neurotics should be corrected when they are in the wrong, and you can correct them in public whenever you want, particularly so when you are in the right. Being in an age-discrepant relationship with an older woman is not a sign of neurosis, incidentally. (Cramer)

Why Men And Women React Differently

Different types of men and women will react in different ways to seeing younger men dating women older than themselves.

Men in general, with an occasional neurotic exception, will not care, or at least will not usually visibly react to seeing you involved with an older woman, and will not see it as a matter that elicits any sort of concern, let alone hostility, on their part. They may know some other man who is dating, or has married, an older woman, but the issue will generally mean little or nothing to them.

Some men may have once harbored, or maybe even still harbor, a fantasy about dating an older woman themselves, and may feel a sense of gratuitous satisfaction at seeing some other man doing that very thing. We watch movies and television shows about heroes who engage in various sorts of adventures and exploits in part because we have the ability to mentally project ourselves into that hero's adventures and exploits, an ability known as identification. This just means that you can see yourself doing the same sort of thing as he does, or at least fantasize that you might possibly be able to do the same thing he does.

A very small number of men might express opposition to seeing you visibly involved with an older woman on the bogus grounds that it is not "normal" or not "natural," which means that they are irrationally projecting the incest taboo onto a relationship where it does not exist in fact. This is just one person's opinion, and you can take it or leave it behind you in the dust as you walk away from men who espouse such opinions. Such opinions are not reflections of reality, they are simply expressions of deep-seated neuroses that reflect the turmoil in their minds, and such opinions are similar to the rantings of alcoholics. Such men are often sexually frustrated and neurotically jealous of other men who have actually accomplished what they have not been able to accomplish because of their self-imposed neurotic inhibitions. Opinions are not reality.

One particular group of men are radically more likely to express opposition to you dating or marrying an older woman – relatives and ex-relatives of a particular older woman with whom you might be involved. Younger male relatives will sometimes be unable to identify with you being involved with their mother or aunt or whatever, particularly in the case of an older woman who has sons your own age. However, a failure on their part to identify with you dating their mother is not an obligation on your part to defer or knuckle under to their failure to understand. If your behavior does not conform to their opinions, your life will nevertheless go on without a hitch. You are free to disregard them and their opinions as you wish. If they can't get used to you dating their mother, you still don't have to care. They may be used to thinking of their mom as a woman who was married to an older man, but neither she nor you need to change your life because some person or group happens to think of you in a different way than the way you think of each other. Opinions held by other people are not obligations for you to live up to those opinions.

The same applies to ex-husbands. Once a woman gets divorced, she is free to date and marry whomever she wants with complete disregard for the opinions, or even the existence, of the ex-husband with whom she

101

decided to part ways. Interestingly, one common cause of divorce is the husband deciding to have an affair with a woman younger than his wife. After such couples divorce, the wife naturally feels that she can do the same as he did to her, and is free to try out dating a younger member of the opposite sex. Some older women like the way such relationships make them feel, and want to make sure that they keep getting those good feelings on a regular basis. If their ex-husbands don't like it, those ex-wives couldn't care less.

The Opinions And Reactions
Of Younger Women

Younger women are a completely different ball of wax. Women see both the idea and the reality of men dating women older than themselves quite differently than men. The rule of thumb is that women under the age of forty, and women of any age who have few prospects of finding male companionship, will express different combinations of shock, resentment and opposition to the idea of older women being involved with younger men.

Younger women, here meaning unmarried women under the age of forty, compete with other women for the attention of single men in their own age range. They do this because they want to get married or get into relationships of some sort that they hope might lead to marriage. The most common way that women compete with other women is to differentiate themselves from each other, most often through the use of visual cues such as clothing, hairstyles, makeup and jewelry. Each woman seeks to customize her appearance using visual cues, and secondary cues that appeal to other senses, such as perfume, so as to present herself in public as a one-of-a-kind package that will appeal to men. Women know that men go for "types" of women, which often means a physical type, such as a tall, thin blonde, so many women surround themselves with "noncompetitive" girlfriends who are different physical types than they are themselves, such as a tall, willowy blonde pairing off with a short, muscular brunette. Each type of woman aims herself at a different "type" of man who prefers a certain physical type of woman, or so the women think.

Single younger woman generally expect themselves to be socially targeted for relationships by single younger men, and single younger women compete with a pool of other single younger women whose physical and social assets are generally similar to their own, no matter how much individual women might try to differentiate themselves with clothing and fashion accessories. Twenty-five year old women share many similarities along physical, social, intellectual and sexual dimensions. They also share similar limitations. There are limits to how mature or sexually experienced a twenty-five year old woman can be, since some things require a substantial number of years to develop.

Younger women like it when most of their fellow female competitors for men in their own age range offer those men pretty much the same things as they do themselves, and younger women who exhibit variations from the norm exhibit variations that nevertheless generally remain within parameters well-known to younger women as a group, such as one woman having a somewhat better education than another young woman.

Women as a group are known to do strange things, or at least things that seem strange to men, to keep other women in line with the group ethos for acceptable behavior and appearance. Women can come down hard on other women if they appear to be violating the group consensus on appearance, such as walking up to women who are total strangers and telling them that their hair or dress is not up to snuff. The younger they are, the more women do things like this. Women compete with other women for male attention, and they want everybody else to be competing on something like the same basis.

There are exceptions, of course. A woman who somehow moves out in front of the crowd, such as a beauty queen winner, will find other women whispering behind her back that they wish that they could scratch her eyes out. In the neurotically jealous eyes of those other women, she has gone "too far" for them to compete with, so they take potshots at her. A woman who goes to the other extreme, such dressing in a slovenly manner, will similarly find herself to be the center of different sorts of unwanted attention from other women.

Younger single women as a group don't like new and unexpected sorts of competition for men popping up, though they have no problem whatsoever dealing with social opportunities and contexts that feature large numbers of men competing with other men for the attention of small numbers of women, as might happen with female students at an engineering college with a predominantly male student body.

Men are free to deliberately choose to associate with types of women that various other types of women will condemn on bogus grounds, the real reason behind their bogus condemnation being that don't like "unfair" competition and will denigrate any other "types" of women that they see as having any sort of competitive edge that men see as a positive competitive edge. Just because a woman is a different type of woman than what other women insinuate should be "your type," their opinions are no reason for you to change anything about the way you think and act. Other women's opinions are not a valid reason for you to refrain from getting involved with the older woman of your choice. You can do whatever you want, starting with laughing off the unsolicited opinions of younger women whom you have rejected as companions. No matter how vehement their self-opinion polls, their opinions do not control the universe or much of anything outside of the confines of their voice boxes. If someone else's opinions don't make you feel good about yourself, you are free to exclude them from your life.

Exactly what it about older women that younger women do not want you to find out about? They don't want you to find out that you don't have to settle for what younger women offer. A younger woman whose sexual experiences have been limited or nonexistent doesn't want you to have a really good time in bed with an woman older than yourself who has years, or decades, of marital sexual experiences to her name, to say nothing of almost the same number of years of expertise at trying to make relationships work. When a younger woman is either worried that she can't compete, or knows for sure that she can't compete, she denigrates, either directly or obliquely, with broad strokes, whatever category of women it is that she is unable to compete with for male attention, particularly where sex is involved. People who can't make the grade always try to cut down their competition, but even such sticks and stones will not cut the competition down.

Women will do this with any category of women (other than the category they themselves are in) that they perceive as unwanted, excessively high-powered competition. This is known to happen when certain types of women are trying to market themselves to men who actually prefer a different type, or types, of women, such as servicemen who choose to date and marry women of the countries where they were stationed while in the service. This both takes those specific men "out of circulation" back home and sets an example that other men might just happen to decide to follow, making the social situation even tougher for the women who get left behind by men they wish were their type.

Women like to say that all's fair in love and war, while conveniently forgetting that all's fair in love and war when men feel like doing it as well. Men like you can associate with an adult older woman, or adult older women, of any type you feel like, particularly so when other women, younger and older, disapprove of your choices. Your life is yours to do with as you wish. Keep in mind that that their disapproval of your choices of female companionship is simply their personal opinion of you doing something that fails to benefit them.

The reality is that it does not matter whether women you don't care for disapprove of your choice of female companionship, as long as you approve of it and you feel good about what you are doing. If it makes you feel good, go out and do it, and if women you have rejected say that they are of the opinion that you should not feel good about what actually does make you feel good, you are still free to keep doing what you like as long as you enjoy yourself. Rationality goes out the back door, and lies come in the front door, when scorned women perceive their personal interests being ignored or thwarted by men who have rejected them. As long as you are having a good time, however, the opinions and interests of women you have rejected nevertheless still mean nothing of consequence.

CHAPTER FIVE
Dating And Sex With Older Women

Conduct Counts

Your conduct counts for a lot when you date older women. This means that the way that you behave when interacting with them determines what they will wind up thinking of you and whether or not a relationship will continue beyond an initial encounter or a first date.

Older women who got divorced got their divorces in large part because something went wrong with their marriages. Often they just didn't like the way their husbands treated them. Their husbands cheated on them, took them for granted, never did any nice little things like bring them flowers now and then, holding doors open for them and generally stopped being sweet and romantic, possibly because they were not all that much in love with them to start with.

After you talk with an older woman for an hour or so, you should be able to get a handle on what she is looking for and what she was disappointed to not have gotten in the past. Just pay attention and get used to reading between the lines of what she says. If an older woman that her ex-husband was always tired, that really means that he was in such bad physical condition that sex required a superhuman effort on his part, which made sex the rarest of events, as opposed to a regular event, in her life. Pay attention to what she says, and you will have a pretty good idea regarding how to conduct yourself when you are with her.

For example, if she talks about how her ex-husband didn't respect her, start holding doors open for her. If an older woman says that she got divorced because her ex was playing around, that really means that she is looking for a guy who has monogamous tendencies. If she says that she doesn't like to cook, that really means that she likes to eat out in restaurants. If she says that she is into exercising, that just might actually mean that sex is her favorite indoor sport. If she doesn't mention her kids, they've either moved out, they go to college out of town or they have formed families of their own, and she may be looking for a full-time live-in companion to alleviate her symptoms of empty-nest syndrome. If she comments on your physique, she is most likely thinking about how she can better study the details of your musculature up close and personal every night.

As far as respect goes, respect means that you should behave as if she is important to you. If she isn't important to you, move on. Do it right, or don't bother trying to get involved at all. You cannot behave with a woman who is ten or more years older than you are as you do with a young woman your own age. Older women are different. Things like drinking marathons, jokes intended for male ears only, clothing with beer company logos or off-color slogans on them and similar activities may seem boyishly amusing to a woman twenty years old, but will fall flat as a pancake with someone who has a substantial age advantage on you. If something wouldn't fly with your mother and her best friends, it probably won't fly with older women in general. An older woman may see such behavior on your part as evidence that you either do not respect her or that you are not mature enough to have a truly adult relationship with her. Some older women might even classify you as the brother-in-spirit of their ex-husbands, as might happen if both you and he celebrate being married to the bottle.

It's okay to help an older woman celebrate her birthday. Celebrate her birthday, but don't bring up her age. This applies to your interactions with older women in general. Don't harp on the age difference. Just accept it as something that happens to exist, like a difference in height or eye color, and move on from there. After the two of you become more comfortable with each other, you might gradually and casually move into discussions with each other about your age difference, but this something to be approached gradually and organically, meaning that this subject is something that should come up naturally in the course of events, and not something that you should suddenly slam on the table.

Women don't like to be constantly reminded of their age after they hit age thirty-five or so, especially when they are currently single. The reason for this is that women, rightly or wrongly, assume that their charms fade with age. Charms and beauty, of course, are in the eyes of the beholder, meaning your eyes. It does charm an older woman to know that you prefer her to younger women, but some older women might be worrying in the back of their minds that you will lose interest with the passage of time. There are no guarantees in real life, however, for men or women. The other side of the coin is that she could lose interest in you if she meets another guy she likes better. Women have been known to expect things of men that they are not themselves offering to those same men.

People of all ages move in and out of relationships all of the time, but an older woman might have a sneaking suspicion that that a younger man's reactions to her age permeates all of his thoughts about, and interactions with, her. At the end of the day, respect is one of the major ways that an older woman measures, and reassures herself about, your interest in her. The greater the extent to which you demonstrate the usual measures of respect for her, the more you assuage her subconscious worries. So go out and respect her. Just make sure that respect is a two-way street

One of the most important ways that you can show that you respect her is to not publicly show any sort of embarrassment about being seen in public with her. Public opinion polls are not the way that a psychologically adult male should go about deciding who to date or not date, and are not something that you should consider in deciding how you express that you like a woman, be it in private or public. If other people look shocked, quizzical or disapproving when they see you with an older woman, their opinions – as expressed in their expressions, reactions and comments – should not influence, guide or otherwise control the way you think and act with a lady who happens to be older than you.

Public opinion polls are conducted by business organizations and political campaigns seeking to measure and understand public opinion to determine whether or not the public approves or disapproves of either what they are doing or planning to do. Conducting polls is one technique used towards these ends. You do not need to conduct a public opinion poll about your relationship because you do not need to be responsive to public opinion or to care about public opinion in the first place. You are not a candidate for public office and you are not selling a product to the public. You can live as you want in the face of public opinion and public disapproval. You are a private individual getting on with your private life in the manner that you prefer and enjoy.

Any number of younger men probably back off from pursuing relationships with older women because they fear public disapproval, which comes down to being afraid of what other people think. Older women sometimes do similar things, saying bizarre things like they couldn't consider getting involved with a younger man because their relatives would have them committed. There is, of course, no legal basis whatsoever for such a thing ever actually happening solely on the basis of age differences. The reality is that public opinion, also known as other people's thoughts, is a will-of-the-wisp, a foggy phantom whose lack of substance becomes readily apparent when you try to grab hold of it and find that it is no more tangible than fog, so huff and puff and watch the fog blow away from your relationship.

Public disapproval is all bark and no bite. Nothing will happen to you if other people disapprove of you being in a relationship with an older woman. Admittedly, some people might make a few facial expressions, comments and characterizations that you don't care for, but, unlike sticks and stones, disapproving faces and whispered comments will never hurt you, because other people's opinions are only opinions, and opinions are thoughts, meaning foggy phantoms that you can walk away from or ignore whenever you feel like it.

You are not a product being offered for sale to the public or a candidate for public office, so whatever sort of informal, spur-of-the-moment public opinion poll that the people near you on the street feel like conducting regarding you and your relationship has not been commissioned by you. It consists of someone else's opinion poll of people who need not concern you, and whose opinions similarly need not concern you. If you did to sign up to hear their opinions, you don't have to care about them. You are too important to care about public opinion, especially the unsolicited public opinions of people you do not care about. You did not solicit other people's opinions because you did not care about them in the first place. Other people's beliefs, opinions and traditions are not the matters you have chosen to consider, so you can ignore them whenever you feel like it.

You don't have to become a passive shock absorber for public opinion. One clever all-purpose comeback or response to hearing somebody say something about you that you do not like about your age-difference relationship is to say out loud "that's the stupidest thing I've ever heard." Keep repeating this louder and louder each time whenever you hear someone say something that you don't like. This sentence is a common form of disapproval used in the software industry, by the way. Repetition breeds confidence on your part, and your preferences, choices and state of mind are more important than other people's opinions.

Feel free to generate some shocks of your own (besides being seen in public with an older woman) by pushing back with your own opinions. Another line you can use is "don't contradict me." If other people don't like your opinions, they don't have to notice. It's up to them to get accustomed to you. You don't have to get along with people you disagree with, and don't have to waste your time thinking about them or their opinions when you can spend your time in the manner of your choosing. Pushing back against other people's opinions will also work out to your advantage in a relationship with an older woman by helping to create a favorable opinion of you in her mind because you took a public stand in favor of your relationship. Doing this when you are dating an older woman both shows her that you respect her and that you are comfortable with being in a relationship with her.

Being romantic is another form of respectful conduct with emotional overtones. Flowers, candlelight dinners, little gifts and so on are always acceptable to older women after you get to know them. Failing to ever engage in such behavior with an older woman might be interpreted by her as a lack of interest on your part, along with a lack of adult social skills, and possibly even a lack of commitment strikingly reminiscent of her ex-husband lack of commitment. Remember that she divorced her ex-husband for reasons that made sense to her, and his lack of respect for her, as evidenced in his conduct, was probably the major factor that led to their divorce. Respect her in public and private and you will be off to a good start. Respect is a good asset to bring to any relationship, so bring as much as you can carry with you. Bring some romance to the table when the two of you sit down for dinner.

Don't be nervous when going out on a date with an older woman. Nervousness means showing that you are worried about something, such as the possibility of public disapproval. Public disapproval is really nothing to be nervous about, because the opinions of people on the street do not add up into anything that is worth your while to have. Their opinions have no meaning or value as regards your relationship.

Older women will see outwardly obvious signs of nervousness as an indicator that you might not have what it takes to cope with an older woman/younger man relationship. When you go out on dates, a few people will point, stare, snicker and whisper and nothing more than that will happen.

After a while, nervousness should cease to be a reaction that being seen dating an older woman elicits. Nervousness is just temporary baggage that comes with learning the game, and it is baggage that you can leave at home instead of bringing it with you when you go outside.

The Marriage Issue

Some older women want to remarry, some do not want to remarry and some do not even think about the issue. Like marriage at any age, it is something to be resolved on a case-by-case basis. There is no one rule that applies to everybody.

There is one thing that you can be sure of in the case of any older woman who is actually looking to marry a younger man. Ninety-nine percent of the time she is looking for an exciting sex life with a younger man, and she's looking for that very specific thing in total disregard for the opinions of the rest of the world, which is often of the opinion that she should not be looking for what it is that she really wants out of life.

A woman who is looking to marry a younger man, especially after menopause, is looking for a relationship that meets her self-defined needs, and that inevitably comes down to having an exciting sex life and the sort of male companionship that will help make her sex life as enjoyable and regular as possible.

Sometimes a divorced woman past the age of forty will be willing to seek out marriage to a younger man, but will also be seeking a much younger man who is available to work full-time, or even work more than full time, so that the older woman can stay home and raise adopted children. Such a woman may be indulging a personal fantasy along the lines of wanting to go back in time and relive her life along the lines of what she wishes had been, as opposed to what actually did happen to her. You have your fantasies, she has hers.

Many younger men are interested in older women in part because many older women are over forty, and therefore past the age where they are likely to get pregnant. If a woman over the age of forty decides that she wants to stop working and adopt kids, that is an issue that a younger man who is completely uninterested in having or raising children needs to find out about and grapple with as soon as possible so that he can decide whether or not he wants to pull the plug on such a relationship. Not all relationships with older women will necessarily turn out to be matches made in heaven of the men involved.

A lot of younger men have noticed that older women are generally easier to along with than is the case for younger woman. They are easier to get along with because they have developed polished social skills as a byproduct of years, or decades, of interacting with men. As a general rule, older women who have been married really are a lot easier to get along with than is the case for younger women, at least most of time.

A forty-five year old woman who was married for twenty years knows from experience exactly what a younger man who is age twenty-five, thirty or whatever, is probably like based on years of marital experiences and from observing her husband's buddies from work and the neighborhood. This is known as cumulative experience. The more experience you have accumulated doing something, the better you will be able to do it. Women who have been married, or have been in long-term relationships for many years, tend to be better at relationships with men than women who have not had those sorts of experiences.

This is no different than somebody who is new on a job and a person who has been on the same job for twenty years: they approach what they do differently because they have different levels of experience guiding their efforts. Each individual will handle the job differently as a result of the differences in cumulative experience. Somebody who's been there and done that already is able to foresee certain types of problems and situations, knows how to react, knows lots of little things than can help keep a marriage, relationship and a household going, and can generally make it easier for both partners to stay interested. Someone who hasn't done those sorts of things will be less able to improvise as well as the person who has had years of very similar experiences.

By contrast, an older woman who was never married or in any number of long-term relationships offers a younger man a different package of benefits in a relationship. She may retain some of aspects of the personality type of younger woman who wanted to get married but never quite got there and, as a consequence, may have unrealistic expectations for a relationship with a younger man as well as a very small reservoir of relevant experiences to draw on for guidance. Finally, she may lack many of the social skills a woman can acquire only in a marriage or as a byproduct of years of long-term, live-in relationships.

A younger woman who worked at getting married might have subsumed some types of interests for the sake of pursuing other types of interests. A good example is the common sort of situation where a younger woman married a man who was not the best sexual match for her because her parents repeatedly suggested that because he had a job and an income high enough to guarantee certain things to her and their children-to-come, or even because her girlfriends told her that he was a good match, at least in their opinion (though not necessarily hers).

An older woman who remembers her mistakes is unlikely to repeat them, and may often be more likely to veer in the opposite direction. If she married a man older than herself the first time around, and that guy later cheated on her with a younger woman, she will feel free to proceed to get involved with, and even marry, a man younger than herself after her divorce comes through or after the child support runs out.

It is a fact that older women who remarry after getting a divorce are seven times more likely to remarry a younger man if they get married a second time than was the case the first time around. When deferring to other people's opinions has produced bad results, older women are more likely to think only of their own opinions and what they want for themselves, rather than what others say they should want. If they are going to make mistakes, it might as well be their own mistakes, since they are the ones who pay the bills. If it turns out for the best, so much the better for them.

A remarriage to a younger man is thus likely to come about for the exclusive purpose of self-satisfaction and to exclude anything that might interfere with the pursuit of that self-satisfaction, meaning an exciting sex life.

The other side of the coin is that the younger man who is not seen as sexually exciting will not get very far with most older women. A very tiny number of older women are looking for younger husbands to be their nonsexual companion, but there is no statistical hard evidence of this beyond tenth-hand anecdotes and rumors.

Women who complain endlessly about their ex-husbands should be avoided because they are living in the past as an escape from a present-day reality that may not be very exciting. An older woman would soon dump a younger man who talked incessantly about his ex-girlfriend, and the younger man is free to dump the older woman who talks incessantly about her ex-husband.

Research About
Older Woman/Younger Man Couples

Happiness is a slippery term, the meaning of which can vary from one person to the next depending on how the individual in question defines happiness for themselves. Satisfaction is the term commonly used in studies that try to get a handle on how people characterize the quality of their relationships. One group of researchers found in one study that both the men and the women in relationships where the women were older were high in satisfaction (Lehmiller).

Another study found that women in relationships with younger men were both more romantically satisfied and committed to their relationships than were women who were involved with men who were older than themselves or with men who were close to their own age. (Lehmiller) An earlier study concluded that there was no statistically significant difference in marital quality between older woman/younger man marriages and age-similar marriages, and there were fewer sexual problems than with age-similar and husband-older marriages. (Vera, Berardo and Berardo; Berardo, Appel and Berardo)

When people respond to surveys, they have been known to respond in socially acceptably ways, meaning that they might often be telling the truth, but not the entire truth. Psychological and sociological surveys and interviews are no different. Social science surveys and research interviews with age-discrepant couples are useful for uncovering general information about how the people in such relationships are faring. The problem is that many people are not really all that comfortable revealing the details of their innermost secrets to strangers conducting surveys and interviews, even if the researchers are legitimate and promise anonymity.

In addition, the surveys and interviews that academic types develop are not really designed to measure certain types of things that are really at the heart of the matter for the people in age-discrepant relationships. The end result is that the researchers leave certain concepts, questions and answer choices out of their experimental design, and respondents either exclude certain things from their answers or use unusually vague euphemisms to characterize their relationships.

Academic research concerning age-discrepant couples has produced results that provide examples of this principle in action. When women who have been in age-discrepant relationships are interviewed or surveyed about the quality of those relationships, certain specific words and phrases keep popping up. Women involved with younger men often say that being with such men makes them feel "young" or "younger." (Proulx)

Obviously, it is physically impossible for a woman to actually become physically younger simply because she is in a relationship with a younger man. These oblique references actually mean that those women involved with younger men are experiencing intense sexual thrills with a younger man that they choose to characterize as making them feel "young" or "younger" because they are reminiscent of the sexual thrills those women experienced when they were younger. These women also say that they find younger men highly attractive, and appearance is both a function of good general health, one component of which is male hormones.

The Real Reasons Why Older Women Enjoy Sex With Younger Men So Much

Remember that the female sense of smell, also know as the olfactory sense is linked to the brain's limbic system, which controls emotions, including mood. The smell of male sweat is known to improve female mood, reduce tension and increase relaxation, most likely through effects on the female neuroendocrine system.

In general, the sweat of a clean and healthy male produces a measurable subconscious emotional enhancement effect on women. Younger men probably produce this effect to the degree to which they are in good general health. Men of any age who are not in good general health will fail to produce this effect on women to the degree to which they are not in good general health. If you're not healthy, your sweat will be unhealthy for your relationship. (Bhutta, Preti)

Male semen contains a variety of biological components other than sperm, including testosterone, estrogen and the thirteen different prostaglandins. (Robertson) The human female vagina absorbs these hormonal components of semen. Female absorption of these hormones found in male semen improves female mood and operates to counteract depression, most likely through effects on neurotransmitters. (Ney) estrogen is specifically known to improve mood in women past the age of menopause. (Coope)

Women who engage in protected sex when men use condoms do not absorb these hormonal components of semen and have been shown to become prone to depression. (Gallup) Female absorption of the hormones found in seminal fluids in this manner produces a variety of positive effects on mood and other aspects of psychological functioning, and these psychological effects persist even after menopause, because the vaginal absorption system continues to function even after pregnancy is no longer possible.

Male bodily functions and hormone levels change with age. The younger a man is, the higher his hormone levels will be in comparison with an unhealthy older man. Hormones means testosterone, estrogen and the various prostaglandins found in male semen. Thus, when an older woman has sex with a man who is substantially younger, she will often be heard to say that she feels younger when with her younger male partner.

What such a woman is really saying is that the elevated levels of testosterone, estrogen and assorted prostaglandins in her male companion's semen make her feel happier by virtue of biochemically enhancing her mood, warding off depression and, last but not least, generally enhancing intercourse. A younger man who happens to be in good health probably has higher absolute levels of these hormones than might an unhealthy older man, further enhancing the older woman's sexual experience and his own sexual experiences, and the fact that he is not a dud will also enhance the way an older woman will perceive him. Sex with younger men thus provides both a variety of both physical and psychological benefits to older women.

STATISTICS ABOUT OLDER WOMAN-YOUNGER MAN COUPLES

"Married Couple Family Groups"

	Number	Percent
Total Married Couples	59,528,000	100.00%
Wife 2-3 years older than husband	4,188,000	7.0%
Wife 4-5 years older than husband	1,856,000	3.1%
Wife 6-9 years older than husband	1,551,000	2.6%
Wife 10-14 years older than husband	553,000	0.9%
Wife 15-19 years older than husband	164,000	0.3%
Wife 20+ years older than husband	183,000	0.3%

Total Age Difference Married Couples
(Older Woman/Younger Man Couples)
  8,475,000 *14.2%*

Total Age Difference Married Couples
4 or More Years Older
(Older Woman/Younger Man Couples)
  4,287,000 *7.2%*

Source: *Current Population Survey (CPS)*
March 2006 "America's Families And
Living Arrangements" "Table FG3.
Married Couple Family Groups"
www.census.gov

"Opposite Sex Unmarried Partner Households"

	Number	Percent
Total Unmarried Households	5,012,000	100.0%
Female 2-3 years older than male	340,000	6.8%
Female 4-5 years older than male	288,000	5.8%
Female 6-9 years older than male	253,000	5.1%
Female 10-14 years older than male	138,000	2.8%
Female 15-19 years older than male	40,000	0.8%
Female 20+ years older than male	19,000	0.4%

Total Age Difference Unmarried Couples (Older Woman/Younger Man Couples)
1,078,000   21.7%

Total Age Difference Unmarried Couples 4 or More Years Older (Older Woman/Younger Man Couples)
738,000   14.9%

Source: Current Population Survey (CPS) March 2006 "America's Families And Living Arrangements" "Table UC3. Opposite Sex Unmarried Partner Households"   www.census.gov

REFERENCES

Felix M. Berardo, Jeffrey Appel and Donna H. Berardo "Age Dissimilar Marriages: Review And Assessment" *Journal Of Aging Studies* 1993, Volume 7, Number 1, pages 93-105.

Monica Boyd and Annie Li "May-December: Canadians In Age-Discrepant Relationships" *Canadian Social Trends* Autumn, 2003, pages 29-33.

Mahmood F. Bhutta "Sex And The Nose: Human Pheromonal Responses" *Journal Of The Royal Society Of Medicine* June, 2007, Volume 100, Number 6, pages 268-274.

William R. Bytheway "The Variation With Age Of Age Differences In Marriage" *Journal Of Marriage And The Family*, November, 1981, Volume 43, Number 4, pages. 923-927.

Census Bureau. United States Department Of Commerce. "America's Families And Living Arrangements." "Table FG3. Married Couple Family Groups" *Current Population Survey (CPS) March 2006.* www.census.gov

Census Bureau. United States Department Of Commerce. "America's Families And Living Arrangements." "Table UC3. Opposite Sex Unmarried Partner Households" *Current Population Survey (CPS) March 2006.* www.census.gov

Jean Coope "Hormonal And Non-Hormonal Interventions For Menopausal Symptoms" *Maturitas: Journal Of The Climacteric & Menopause 1996, Volume* 23, pages 159-168.

Duncan Cramer "Personality, Socioeconomic Status And Age Disparity In Marriage" *Personality And Individual Differences* 1993, Volume 15, Number 6, pages 125-121.

Gordon G. Gallup, Jr., Rebecca L. Burch and Steven M. Platek "Does Semen Have Antidepressant Properties?" *Archives Of Sexual Behavior* June, 2002, Volume 31, Number 3, pages 289-293.

Erving Goffman *Stigma: Notes On The Management Of Spoiled Identity* 1963, Simon And Schuster.

Ariane Kemkes-Grottenthaler "For Better Or Worse, Till Death Us Do Part: Spousal Age Gap And Differential Longevity: Evidence From Historical Demography" *Collegium Antropologicum* 2004, Volume 28, Supplement 2, pages 203-219.

Justin J. Lehmiller and Christopher R. Agnew "Marginalized Relationships: The Impact Of Social Disapproval On Romantic Relationship Commitment" *Personality And Social Psychology Bulletin* January, 2006, Volume 32, Number 1, pages 40-51.

Justin J. Lehmiller and Christopher R. Agnew "Commitment In Age-Gap Heterosexual Romantic Relationships: A Test Of Evolutionary And Socio-Cultural Predictions" *Psychology of Women Quarterly* 2008, Volume 32, pages 74-82.

Lord and Thomas *Real Salesmanship In Print: Strategy In Advertising* 1911, pages 41-44.

Sarah Mahoney "Seeking Love" *AARP: The Magazine* November-December, 2003. Statistics from: "Lifestyles, Dating And Romance: A Study Of Midlife Singles." Xenia P. Montenegro, study conducted for the AAARP, September, 2003. www.aarp.org

P.G. Ney "The Intravaginal Absorption Of Male Generated Hormones And Their Possible Effect On Female Behaviour" *Medical Hypotheses* 1986, Volume 20, pages 221-231.

Emma Otta, Beatriz Barcellos Pereira Lira, Nadia Maria Delavati, Otavio Pimenti Cesar and Carla Salati Guirello Pires "The Effect Of Smiling And Of Head Tilting On Person Perception" *The Journal Of Psychology* 1994, Volume 128, pages 323-31.

Gillian Porter, Bruce M Hood, Tom Troscianko and C. Neil Macrae "Females, But Not Males, Show Greater Pupillary Response To Direct-Than Deviated-Gaze Faces" *Perception* 2006, Volume 35, pages 1129-1136.

George Preti, Charles J. Wysocki, Kurt T. Barnhart, Steven J. Sondheimer, and James J. Leyden "Male Axillary Extracts Contain Pheromones That Affect Pulsatile Secretion Of Luteinizing Hormone And Mood In Women Recipients" *Biology Of Reproduction* 2003, Volume 68, pages 2107-2113.

Nichole Proulx, Sandra L. Caron and Mary Ellin Logue "Older Women/Younger Men: A Look At The Implications Of Age Difference In Marriage" *Journal Of Couple & Relationship Therapy* 2006, Volume 5, Number 4, pages 43-64.

Sarah A. Robertson "Seminal Plasma And Male Factor Signaling In The Female Reproductive Tract" *Cell And Tissue Research* 2005, Volume 322, pages 43-52.

Constance L. Shehan, Felix M. Berardo, Hernan Vera and Sylvia Marion Carley "Women in Age-Discrepant Marriages" *Journal Of Family Issues* September, 1991, Volume 12, Number 3, pages 291-305

Scott J. South "Sociodemographic Differentials In Mate Selection Preferences" *Journal Of Marriage And The Family* November, 1991, Volume 53, pages 928-940.

Karine Spiegel, Esra Tasali, Plamen Penev and Eve Van Cauter "Sleep Curtailment In Healthy Young Men Is Associated With Decreased Leptin Levels, Elevated Ghrelin Levels, And Increased Hunger And Appetite" *Annals Of Internal Medicine* December 7, 2004, Volume 141, Number 11, pages 846-850.

Hans P. A. Van Dongen, Greg Maislin, Janet M. Mullington and David F. Dinges "The Cumulative Cost Of Additional Wakefulness: Dose-Response Effects On Neurobehavioral Functions And Sleep Physiology From Chronic Sleep Restriction And Total Sleep Deprivation" *Sleep* 2003, Volume 26, Number 2, pages 117-126.

Hernan Vera, Felix M. Berardo and Donna H. Berardo "On Gold Diggers: Status Gain In Age Heterogamous Marriages" *Journal Of Aging Studies* 1987, Volume 1, Number 1, pages 51-64.

Hernan Vera, Donna H. Berardo and Felix M. Berardo "Age Heterogamy In Marriage" *Journal Of Marriage And The Family*, August, 1985, Volume 47, Number 3, pages 553-566.

www.ingramcontent.com/pod-product-compliance
Lightning Source LLC
Chambersburg PA
CBHW061310280526
45784CB00002B/948